NOURISH

HOLLY DAVIS

NOURISH

HOLLY DAVIS

PHOTOGRAPHS
GEOFF LUNG

STYLING
HOLLY DAVIS AND YOLANDE GRAY

TEN SPEED PRESS

BERKELEY   TORONTO

INTRODUCTION AND ACKNOWLEDGMENTS

When asked, I describe myself as a food-passionate being and I realized quite recently that most of my memories are connected in some way to food. At the age of thirteen I dined with my family in the village of Champagne in France. It was a highly memorable event because of the tremendous argument that broke out over dinner. My parents threatened separation and the entire family ended the evening in tears and distress. Before the fracas, my father told my sister and me that the still "blanc de blanc" Champagne we were about to drink would possibly be the finest wine we would ever be offered, and I can still recollect its flavor. I also recall the sweet taste of parsley, butter and garlic that covered the "praire" (clams) that I had for dinner, and I remember what everyone else ate – but I have no idea what started the argument. This perhaps sums up my relationship to food.

Even my earliest memories are connected in some way to food and I recall many special events by the food that was offered on the occasion. Before he studied the law, my father was a chef at the Trocadero Hotel in Liverpool, England. My mother was the primary cook at home but I remember fondly that on Sundays my father was in charge of the kitchen for dinner, and I also remember the rare occasions he made us toffees and spun us baskets of sugar.

I was born in time for breakfast and took to food with gusto from day one, willing to try almost anything. My culinary interests have taken several turns over the course of my life and what lies between the covers of this book has been influenced by them all.

I was raised in Britain on a typical diet of meat and fresh vegetables, plenty of dairy food, and refined sugar. At fourteen I met Tracy Sohn and her sister Pip. They introduced me to macrobiotics, an Eastern philosophy that describes the order of the universe, and offers ideas such as "you are what you eat." This philosophy felt so right to me I took it home and attempted, in vain, to convince my family it was the only way to live. It was to be the single largest influence on my life so far.

Like so many, I became holier than thou and began a mission to change the world. I felt you were saved if you understood this philosophy and applied it, and damned if you didn't. My family accepted this interest surprisingly well. It was hard for them, particularly my mother, as I took

over the fridge and rejected her offerings frequently. I thank my parents for their acceptance and support. With time and experience I am much more grateful and open to all I am offered.

Good fortune and circumstance led me to Sydney in 1982 after a year in Japan. By 1984 I was the proprietor of my first restaurant, Manna, in Rozelle, Sydney, and this experience was a wonderful teacher. It gave me the opportunity to play, experiment and learn with the help of my loyal customers, who offered constant feedback, and Andrzej Gospodarczyk, from whom I bought the business. With great generosity he passed on much of what he knew.

In 1985 I opened Iku Wholefood in Glebe, Sydney, with my business partner Willem Venter. We worked together for six years developing a business founded on the belief that what you put in at the beginning of a meal is reflected absolutely in the customers' satisfaction at the end.

Willem died in 1991. I thank him for sharing his passion for food with me, for his love and laughter and the creative talent that birthed Iku.

After Willem's death, Ken Israel became my business partner, and to Ken I have a deep gratitude for our friendship, his vision and all that he has taught me about business. Iku is now a well-oiled machine with high standards of production and delivery that make me proud to have been its co-creator.

I sold my share of Iku to Ken in 1997 to write, teach, cater and consult on what I call "real food," a style of food that has been born out of thirteen years of vegan food production.

The principle of real food is to combine simplicity, nourishment, taste, texture and beauty in order to provide the most appropriate food for the circumstance. It is flexible and wide-ranging, drawing on many cultural influences, but bound by none in particular. The recipes in *Nourish* incorporate some animal food as well as fresh fruit and vegetables. The emphasis is on the high quality of ingredients and on the needs of the whole person and the environment. Consequently "real food" nourishes more than the physical being alone.

I would like to acknowledge these people for their contribution to the creation of this book:

My partner, Noek Witzand, and our daughter India, for all their love and support, and for the late nights and early mornings. For all the meals they have tested and all the meals they went without, not forgetting the many hours they have left me alone to create this book.

Jim Wilson at Spiral Foods for his generous support and sponsorship of this project. And also for his commitment to excellence in his business, which is reflected in the products he sells and the service Spiral Foods offers as a distributor of wholefoods in Australia.

My respect and gratitude to Grant Eastwood and Michael Dunne at Macro Wholefoods for their sponsorship of *Nourish* and for the tenacious spirit that has assisted them to create Sydney's finest wholefood outlets. I also acknowledge the long business relationship we have shared.

Yolande Gray for her desire to design this book, for her ability to hold the big picture and make it happen and for the delight I have had in working with her.

To my agent, David Holland, for his trust and tenacious spirit. Publisher Julie Stanton for her belief in this project that has made it a reality. Susan Tomnay and Brigitta Doyle for their careful editing of the manuscript. Geoff Lung for his patience, grace and expertise in taking the photographs. Megan Brown and Mindy Byrne for their willing assistance with the photo shoot and for making it so much fun. Thanks also to Megan for the prawn oil recipe.

I would like to thank Cecille Weldon for the name of this book, her invaluable business advice since I moved on from Iku, her time, her friendship, her oven and the endless meals eaten to test recipes.

Airdre Grant, macrobiotic counselor, cooking teacher and dear friend, for helping me to edit the recipes and for her belief in me and this project.

This book has been for many years a promise to myself and to the devoted customers of Iku Wholefood. To the staff of Iku Wholefood, present and past, and all the customers, I thank you for all the lessons you helped me to learn and for your support and encouragement of the business and of me, through good times and bad.

Nicholas Grey Imeson Coffil, without whom I would still be living in a far-off London town, thank you for starting me off in this land I love so much.

I also acknowledge these people who have taught me so much more about my passion: Siraporn, David Sexton, Michael Doherty, Denis Cullity, Jennifer Byrne, Nancy Byrne, John Downes, Martin Kenrick, Merilee Bennett, Deborah Shaw, Karen Burn, Eben Venter, Dominic Angelucci, Lee Anne Carson, Deborah Preston, Nicholaas van Schalkwvyk, Blair Singer, Robert and Kim Kiyosaki.

Most of the recipes in this collection are easy to make and look appealing without a lot of fuss. Many are made from well-known ingredients and some may introduce you to less well-known items. A glossary (page 33) will explain these new items, their origins and some of their uses.

Where a less well-known ingredient is used, I have tried to include several recipes with that ingredient so it's not left to languish in your cupboards. These recipes will also demonstrate the different ways one ingredient may be used.

I am the sort of cook who works on intuition. I have had cooking disasters, but they have been relatively few because of some simple rules I impose on myself:

- Consider the season and use those ingredients that are currently bountiful.
- Consider the needs of each person to be fed.
- Use the best-quality ingredients affordable at the time.
- Buy from trusted sources; ask questions about the produce and its origins.
- Read labels to determine ingredients and origins.
- Try to avoid products with preservatives, additives and synthetic coloring agents and those with commercial salt and refined sugar.
- Be open to trying almost anything.
- Respect the origin of ingredients, combining those that come from similar climates if not the same place.
- When in doubt keep it simple and do as little as possible to the ingredients.
- Be grateful for the produce you work with. I believe this contributes to your cooking and eating enjoyment.
- Try to create every meal as a special occasion in some way.

There are enormous variables in cooking and I see it as an alchemic art form rather than a domestic science. Please adapt these recipes to suit your needs. Regard the recipes as beginnings. Once you learn the style you can then adapt that style to suit the ingredients you have on hand. Some ingredients are a perfect match for others, which I hope you will discover as you explore these recipes.

EQUIPMENT NEEDS AND CARE

When at home and when advising people on kitchen needs there are a few tools I consider essential. This list covers everything you will need to make the recipes in this book, though some are more important than others.

- A set of good knives: at a minimum a general chopping knife and a small vegetable knife. A cleaver is a handy addition if you eat fowl, as it is ideal for chopping cleanly through their soft bones. Stainless steel is easiest to keep clean and I like a wooden handle. The size and weight of the chopping knife is up to you.
- Sharpening stone.
- Two wooden chopping boards. Use one solely for animal produce, one for fruit and the other side for vegetables; mark them accordingly.
- 4-cup (1-L) , 8-cup (2-L), 12-cup (3-L), 20-cup (5-L) pans made of stainless steel, enamel or cast iron according to your budget; a 9-in (22-cm) deep frying pan with a lid; and a mild steel wok with a stand. You will need a wok with a flat bottom if using an electric stove.
- A stainless steel steamer for grains and vegetables that can go on top of or within another pot.
- Bamboo steamers of various sizes to use with the wok (not essential).
- A 12-cup (3-L) stainless steel pressure cooker.
- A large colander.
- A large and a small sieve (one large will do).
- Wooden stirring spoons, a flat rice paddle and long wooden chopsticks.
- Metal spoons and spatulas.
- A metal whisk.
- A rolling pin.
- A sisal brush (or other scrubbing brush) for washing vegetables.
- A good vegetable peeler.
- A zester.
- A grater with small and large grates.
- A ginger grater.
- Measuring cups and spoons.
- A blender, preferably with a glass jug.
- A food processor. Or make do with a blender or a blending wand.
- Cake pans.
- Baking sheets.
- A brush for oiling pans, another dry brush (parchment paper can substitute).
- Timer.
- Containers in various shapes and sizes with lids for storing cooked food, preferably in stainless steel, glass or enamel.
- Parchment paper for wrapping dry food.
- The secret ingredient: enjoy what you are doing, however repetitive it may be, relax and have fun.

A NOTE ABOUT PLASTICS

Plastics release gas and can contaminate food. I cover a bowl with a plate or use a sheet of unbleached paper to create a seal over a sauce.

CARE OF EQUIPMENT

Maintaining an orderly space seems to be the best way to ensure equipment is not lost or broken. Here are a few things to consider in the care of basic equipment:
- Never use knives to open tins or jars.
- Do not twist knives when cutting large pumpkins.
- Wipe chopping boards and put a handful of salt in the center. Rub this into the board and leave for 5 minutes, wash well in cold water and leave upright to dry away from direct heat.

SHARPENING YOUR KNIVES

There are many types of knives and it's a good idea to check the best way to sharpen them when you buy them.

- I use a sharpening stone, found in good kitchen shops or hardware stores.
- Put the stone in cold water for 5 minutes before using it.
- Hold the stone in one hand and the knife in the other under cold running water.
- With the knife on the stone at an angle of approximately 45 degrees, move the knife in small circles, working your way up and down the stone and the blade to ensure the whole knife is equally sharp. Sharpen one side then the other (except with Japanese knives which are only sharpened on one side). There is no need to apply pressure to the blade.
- Test the blade's sharpness by cutting a tomato or other soft vegetable.
- Clean the blade before using again.
- Wash the stone to remove any buildup of metal filings, dry and store.
- Once the knife is very sharp you can keep it that way by using a steel once or twice a week, depending on how much use it gets.
- To keep knives sharp, store separately.

HYGIENE AND SAFETY WHEN HANDLING FOOD

There are regulations commercial kitchens must adhere to in order to safeguard against large-scale contamination. This is perhaps obvious but I believe it is important to take care at home too.

PERSONAL

Tie back long hair, wear an apron and wash your hands well before and during preparation; keep separate dish towels handy to dry your hands.

PREPARATION AREA
- Use separate cloths for counters, hands and floor, and change cloths regularly.
- Keep separate chopping boards for meat, vegetables and fruit.
- Clean chopping boards with salt once a week.

- Always use oven mitts when using the oven.
- Never use damp oven mitts or dish towels to pick up hot dishes.

FOOD
- To prevent cross contamination, clean your hands well after handling fish, eggs, or meat, and before handling any other raw or cooked ingredients.
- Keep all produce that needs refrigeration below 41°F (5°C) before and after preparation.
- Thaw all frozen produce in the refrigerator.
- Never refreeze any produce.
- Ensure the blood from fish and meat is kept completely contained if there is other raw produce in the refrigerator or nearby.
- Cut mold from hard cheeses, fruit and vegetables and eat the remainder. However, throw out all moldy bread, grains, seeds, nuts, fresh cheese and soy products.
- When deep-frying, always keep a lid or woolen blanket close by to put over the pan in case it ignites. Do not pour water on burning oil as it will explode. Never attempt to move a flaming pan.

HEAT SOURCES

For everyday cooking, a gas flame is my preferred source of heat. With the added benefit of immediate control, gas is the next best thing to cooking over an open fire.

If you happen to cook over an open fire and when barbecuing, remember it is the latent heat within the coals that you want. The flame will burn the food, creating toxicity. Make a hot fire, allow the coals to build up, then rake off the burning timber and cook over the glowing embers. When cooking in this way if oil or fat drops onto the fire, flames may be created. Blow these out right away.

WATER

Water is a fundamental requirement for good health. We use water to cool, moisten, soothe and relax ourselves and since two-thirds of our body's mass is water it makes sense that the quality of the water we drink and use in our cooking is as high as the quality of the other produce we consume.

It has become difficult to determine what is safe water. There is huge controversy over water supply, pollution and the addition of fluoride and chlorine to the common water supply of many cities. I believe it is up to us as individuals to inform ourselves and take steps to make sure the water we drink is pure. There is a large range of water purifiers and filters on the market; choose one that best suits your needs. Paul Pitchford has a section on water in his book, *Healing with Whole Foods*.

Good-quality ingredients are the basis of any dish and they can make the difference between a mediocre and a memorable meal.

No matter what you are looking for, let all your senses play a part in your choice and if it is possible, choose products that have been grown biodynamically or organically. Look for or ask for proof of certification to ensure that you are getting what you are paying for. By buying biodynamic and organic produce you are supporting not only your health and your family's health, but also sustainable farming practices that ensure the best future for those that follow and for the earth that nourishes you.

My preference for biodynamic and organic produce comes from experience. I cook with a minimal amount of spices and strong seasonings so the produce I use needs to be as flavorsome and as alive as possible. I find that the flavor of foods grown without the use of synthetic fertilizers contributes greatly to the success of a meal. If the ingredients have full flavors and great color and texture, not much else is required to make an exceptional meal.

Choosing biodynamic and organic produce will mean you are eating more in accordance with the seasons. A vine-ripened tomato in summer is a heavenly thing, a far cry from the supermarket varieties that are grown in chemicals and sold underripe and tasteless all year round; and a firm, dark orange pumpkin may inspire many a winter meal. Look for vibrant colors, feel the texture, smell the object, and take note of its weight and density.

Read the labels on packaged foods and check the use-by dates. I try to avoid foods with synthetic colorings and preservatives. Buy fresh produce and use it quickly so you will benefit from all the nutrients before they deteriorate.

CHOOSING VEGETABLES
Look for vegetables that
- Have dense, intense colors
- Are firm and rigid
- Have uniform color unless variegated
- Have roots and leaves intact
- Have no evidence of browning or molding, as distinct from blemishes found on some organic vegetables.

CHOOSING EGGS
When fresh they have a metallic smell and the shell is brittle.

CHOOSING SALT
Salt is a controversial ingredient and there are many conflicting opinions and advice on its use. Over-use of salt can be a factor in hypertension (high blood pressure) increasing the risk of heart disease

and strokes. Processed foods such as some breads, dairy products, biscuits, pickles, processed meats and preserves contain large amounts of salt and we can be eating more salt than we realize.

Salt is an essential ingredient for good health. It is obtained from rock deposits, salt springs or the sea. Rock salt is almost pure sodium chloride.

I believe sea salt is the best. It contains many different salts, minerals and trace elements, including potassium, calcium, magnesium, copper, zinc, manganese, iron and iodine, and these are also components of human body tissue.

I use Celtic sea salt. This product has a history that can be traced back to the ninth century. It is a damp, coarse gray sea salt that has a discernable flavor rather than a sharp, salty taste. As it is strong I use less of it.

As a rule it is best to use sea salt in the cooking and preparation of foods rather than on the table as a condiment. This ensures its even distribution and that the amount consumed is minimal. Sea salt helps to soften grains; it brings out the sweetness in cooked fruit and vegetables and enhances flavor.

If you like extra salt, make some gomashio (page 166) to offer as a condiment. There are several other products mentioned in this book that are made with salt. These are umeboshi plums and umeboshi vinegar, tamari, shoyu and miso. Look for those made with sea salt rather than refined salt, to make sure you are getting the best quality available. Ask your supplier if you are unsure.

Cooking in autumn and winter involves a little more salt than in spring and summer. I find a good balance for salt is potassium-rich foods. Eating sweet, potassium-rich foods such as grain sweeteners, maltose, rice syrup, dried fruit, and vegetables like sweet potato and pumpkin may help decrease the desire for excess salty foods.

I like to use several forms of salt in one dish to create a more interesting and complex flavor. If you are doing this, beware the tendency to oversalt. If you do oversalt a dish, it is sometimes possible to correct the balance by adding another ingredient such as lemon juice or vinegar, or something sweet like rice malt or palm sugar. But of course sometimes you will have to start again.

CHOOSING OILS

When choosing oils consider the processing. Unrefined oils are best. Some labels that say cold-pressed may include oils which have been heated and treated with other substances. Oils are referred to as saturated, monounsaturated and polyunsaturated. As saturated oils have been linked to high cholesterol levels, monounsaturates are considered a healthier choice for regular use. Also they do not become rancid as quickly as polyunsaturates.

- When oils are heated they may lose some or all of their nutritional value so it is good to use raw oils in dressings and sauces.
- Avoid allowing oils to become so hot that they smoke and burn as these oils are unhealthy.
- Oils have a limited life so it is best to use them while they are fresh.
- Store oils in dark glass bottles away from direct sunlight, preferably in the refrigerator.

I keep a regular supply of the following oils:
- Extra-virgin olive oil: for general use in salad dressings, over grains and vegetables when baking, and in any dish when it is used raw.
- Virgin olive oil: to cook with generally, to deep-fry and for Mediterranean-style dishes.
- Sesame oil: to sauté Asian-style dishes.
- Toasted sesame oil: added once meal is cooked for flavor. Do not use to cook with.
- Peanut oil: for sautéing and deep-frying (peanut oil has the highest boiling point of all cooking oils so it seals the food quickly and does not burn easily).
- Corn oil: for use in pastries as it adds good color when butter is not used.

I also keep small quantities of
- Walnut oil: for salads and vegetable dishes.
- Almond oil: for baking and salads.
- Apricot kernel oil: for baking and salads.
- Coconut oil: for some baking.
- Essential oils of lemon, lime and orange for dressings, sauces and baking.

A NOTE ABOUT PEANUT OIL
If possible, use organic peanut oil as chemical spraying is common on commercial crops of peanuts.

OILS AND COOKING

WATER-OIL SAUTÉ If you are concerned about the overheating of oils when sautéing, pour a small amount of water in the pan before adding the oil and keep the flame medium. Never add water to heated oil, as it will spit.

DEEP-FRYING The desired effect is to cook the ingredients quickly, sealing in the flavor and retaining the nutritional value of the food.

It is vital that the oil reaches a high enough temperature to seal the food to be fried. If this does not happen, the food absorbs large amounts of oil, making it soggy and greasy. Deep-fried food should be a clean golden-brown, never blackened.

DEEP-FRYING INSTRUCTIONS

- Pour cold oil (use organic peanut oil or virgin olive oil) into a deep, dry pan or wok.
- Heat the oil and test the temperature by dropping a piece of bread or a small amount of the food you are frying into the oil. It should sink to the bottom and then rise quickly to the surface and brown within 8 seconds.
- Once the oil is hot enough, use a slotted spoon with a long handle to carefully lower some of the food into it.
- Remove food from the oil as soon as it is cooked and place immediately on paper towels to drain.
- Use a fine sieve to remove any debris from the oil before continuing to fry the rest of the food.
- Allow the oil to cool completely before moving it.
- Depending on the food you have fried, you may be able to reuse the oil for deep-frying. Pour the cooled oil through a paper filter and add an umeboshi plum to it. The salty plum will attract any remaining impurities and help preserve the oil until further use. Store in a glass bottle in the refrigerator.

CHOOSING SEAFOOD (USE ALL YOUR SENSES)

WHOLE FISH

- Look to see that it is bright and shiny, that the eyes are firm and dark and that the scales are firmly attached.
- If the fish has been gutted, look at the color of the blood. If it is bright red the fish is likely to have been cleaned that day; if the blood is very dark the fish may have been there longer. Ungutted whole fish do not last as long as gutted, so an ungutted fish is often a sign of freshness.
- The flesh of fresh fish bounces back when pressed.
- Use your nose: a fresh fish smells sweet and quite pleasant.

FILLETS

Fillets of fish should be firm when gently pressed, they should also look shiny and bright. Do not buy fillets if they are dull, soft or dry.

When buying fillets, ask to have a whole fish scaled, gutted and filleted and take the head and bones with you for stock. This is the cheapest way to buy fish as it gives you the basis for another meal. Make the stock the same day or the next day, and freeze it once cooled.

SHELLFISH
- Shellfish should be brightly colored with no black areas (unless this is part of their natural coloring).
- Fresh oysters gleam and usually contain seawater.
- Crab is best when bought alive. To kill, place in the freezer for at least an hour before cooking.
- If you buy dead crabs look for those with all their legs attached, clear colors and a fresh smell.
- Fresh prawns are extremely rare. They have a very short life once taken from the ocean and today most are flash frozen on the boats. If these have been well handled they can still be a wonderful addition to a dish.
- Green prawns should be firm when squeezed unless they are tiny school prawns which feel much softer.
- Prawn heads and tails should be firmly attached and the same color as the body.
- Freshly caught prawns are easily identified by their long feelers as these snap off once the prawns are frozen.

If you are ever in Sydney at Christmas time I recommend that you look for Sydney harbor prawns. These are very small and have long tangled feelers. They take longer to peel than king prawns, but they have the sweetest flavor and are well worth the effort. They are wonderful for lunch with fresh bread, mayonnaise and a chunk of cucumber.

BABY OCTOPUS
Choose small, firm, white octopus and prepare in this way:
Wash under cold running water. Cut off the head below the eyes, then cut off the eyes. Cut the head open and remove the innards, wash and dry. Push the beak through the hole in the center of the body. Cut the body in four so there are two legs to a piece.

CHOOSING NOODLES

There are many varieties of noodles. The only ones mentioned here are those used in this book. Experiment with others to find the ones you enjoy most. I like to use the noodles that are traditional with certain dishes, but if you prefer something different there are no rules.
- Noodles are widely available dried and can sometimes be bought fresh. Generally both varieties contain salt. Fresh noodles often also contain preservatives. Look for those that are preservative-free, and if you can find them, buy those made with organically grown ingredients.
- I prefer noodles made from unbleached white flour because wholemeal noodles, though more nutritious, are often rather gritty and it is the smooth texture of noodles that is so inviting.
- It is worth paying for high-quality noodles from reputable distributors. Some cheaper

noodles, particularly rice noodles, can taste of bleach and in others the flour may be stale. Dried noodles can be kept for several months placed in an airtight container in a cool spot.

SOBA NOODLES

Soba is the Japanese word for buckwheat. Soba noodles come in many varieties. They are quite thin and have straight cut edges. They cook in 8 to 12 minutes.

Soba noodles are versatile and can be used in soups, with sauces and in stirfry dishes. They can also be baked in a sauce or fried. Eaten hot or cold, they make a great quick meal.

SOME VARIETIES OF SOBA

- A combination of buckwheat flour and whole-wheat flour in varying proportions.
- 100 per cent buckwheat flour. These need to be carefully cooked as they have a tendency to fall apart while cooking.
- O cha soba (one of my favorites) made with buckwheat flour, wheat flour, and fine ground green tea. These are wonderful eaten cold in summer or in a light broth in autumn and winter.

UDON NOODLES

These noodles are made from wheat flour. They are thicker than soba and have a chewier texture. They cook in approximately 12 minutes.

SOME VARIETIES OF UDON

- Plain udon, made from unbleached white flour.
- Whole-wheat udon.
- Jinenjo udon is a small sticky mountain potato noodle from Japan.
- Brown rice udon is made from a combination of wheat flour and brown rice flour.

SOMEN NOODLES

These are very thin round noodles made from wheat flour. They have a slippery texture, are ideal served cold as a dipping noodle, and they make the fastest one-pot soup. Somen can also be made from unbleached white flour or whole-wheat flour.

SHIRATAKI NOODLES

Found in containers in Japanese food suppliers, these noodles are made from yam paste and are wheat-free. They are clear to white in color and have a chewy jelly-like texture.

BIFUN NOODLES (JAPANESE RICE NOODLES)

A vermicelli-style white rice noodle, they cook in approximately 5 minutes and suit stirfries, soups and broths. They can also be deep-fried for a crispy snack.

ASIAN DRY RICE NOODLES

These come in many styles: flat sticks, round noodles, wide and narrow noodles, thick and thin. Some are short, others long. Choose the ones that appeal to you. They are all fast-cooking.

ASIAN FRESH RICE NOODLES

These are found in Chinese and Asian food stores and some health food shops. Look for the varieties made without preservatives.

When they are very fresh these noodles are soft and flexible. If they are hard they have been refrigerated and should be placed in warm water to soften, so the layers can be separated more easily. Fresh rice noodles come in a range of shapes. Try out a few. I like the wide flat ones that I can cut to suit the dish I am making, and these can also be used to wrap ingredients.

It is best to use fresh noodles within a day or two of buying. Look for any discoloration on the surface of the noodles. If you see any bright pink or yellow spots, do not use the noodles, as this indicates bacteria.

COOKING NOODLES

Noodles are generally quick-cooking; the time required depends on the type of flour used to make the noodle and on its thickness. Remember that noodles absorb a lot of flavor from the ingredients they are cooked with, so if they sit for a long time before serving, check the seasoning.

As a rule the following method works well for those noodles containing wheat flour. The method of refreshing noodles with cold water helps to cook them evenly, making sure the outside is not soft and sticky while the inside remains firm. A well-cooked noodle is silky in the mouth and slightly chewy without being hard.

DRY SOBA AND UDON NOODLES

- Bring plenty of cold water to a rolling boil over high heat.
- Do not add salt to the water if the noodles contain salt already.
- Hold the noodles upright above the water and sprinkle them in a few at a time. If you add them in a clump, they might stick together.
- Use chopsticks or a long fork to stir them and keep them separate.
- Bring the water back to a rolling boil.
- Add 1 cup (8 fl oz/250 ml) cold water or stock to "refresh" the noodles.
- Bring back to a rolling boil and repeat the refreshing process twice more.
- Pour the noodles into a large colander and wash under cold running water to remove any surface starch. The noodles will now feel slippery and be quite shiny to look at.

- To reheat the noodles, place them in a noodle basket or sieve and submerge them in simmering stock or water.
- To serve them cold, drain them well, set aside in a cool place until you need them, then run them under cold water and drain well before serving.

FRESH SOBA AND UDON NOODLES
These will cook a little faster than dry noodles. Follow the same procedure but refresh them twice only.

DRY SOMEN, BIFUN AND THIN RICE NOODLES
Follow the same procedure as for dry soba noodles, but there is no need to refresh these noodles as they are very thin and cook easily.

FRESH RICE NOODLES
To boil:
- Drop into simmering stock 2 minutes before serving as these take very little cooking.
- Do not boil vigorously or they will collapse.

To fry:
- Heat a frying pan or wok, add oil, then the noodles and cook them without stirring, for approximately 7 minutes over medium to high heat.
- Turn them over once they begin to brown and become crisp.
- Add seasonings towards the end of the cooking time.
- Use a flat metal spatula to turn them over.
- Handle gently as they can break apart easily.

CHOOSING SEA VEGETABLES/SEAWEEDS
These useful and intriguing plants come in a variety of shapes, colors and sizes. Those mentioned here are only the varieties that appear in this book. There are others available in good health food stores and Asian suppliers.

Sea vegetables have been widely used by many cultures but are perhaps most commonly associated with Japanese food. Japanese varieties of sea vegetables are now being harvested in South Australia, Tasmania and New Zealand.

Sea vegetables are extremely nutritious, beneficial to health and come in a form that is easily digested. Including small amounts of them regularly as part of a meal can provide vitamins, minerals and amino acids, calcium, iron and iodine to your diet while also creating interest and variety.
- Arame and wakame are higher in calcium than milk.

- Wakame and kombu contain more iron than beef.
- Kombu and arame, depending on the time of harvest, can contain much more iodine than is found in shellfish.

It is easy once one develops a taste for sea vegetables to go a bit wild and to eat lots of them, believing them to be a wonder food. This is not a great idea as the thermal nature of sea vegetables is cooling and they have a high salt content. It is best to use them as side dishes in salads and as condiments. The optimum amount of dried sea vegetables is approximately $\frac{1}{3}$ oz (10 g) per day.

Dried sea vegetables are economical because you use only small quantities at a time. Soak them first in plenty of water to promote faster cooking and easier digestion. When soaked, they expand to varying degrees, depending on the variety. Keep the soaking water from wakame and kombu for stocks; strain it first as it may contain particles of sand and grit. Use the soaking water from arame or hijiki to water plants or to add to the drinking water of pets.

   Dried sea vegetables should be kept in dark glass jars away from direct sunlight. They will keep well for years without deterioration.

Fresh sea vegetables can be stored in glass jars in the refrigerator. Rinse well before use as they are salty and may be gritty.

AGAR-AGAR
Known as kanten in Japan, this is a clear gelatin made from sea vegetables. It is used in sweet and savory dishes, to make jams, fruit jellies, aspics and molds. It contains no calories and is a good source of calcium and iron.

   agar-agar sets at room temperature and may be reheated and reset which makes it much easier to adjust than other setting agents, such as gelatin. More liquid or more dissolved agar may be added as needed. agar-agar can be bought in bars, as a powder or in flakes.

COOKING WITH AGAR-AGAR
- 1 bar or $\frac{1}{4}$ teaspoon powder or 4 tablespoons of the flakes will set 2 cups (16 fl oz/500 ml) liquid.
- agar-agar does not set highly acidic foods such as distilled and wine vinegar, or foods that are high in oxalic acid (spinach or rhubarb). To set these, use Irish moss or carrageen.
- agar-agar is a natural product and subject to variation, so always test-set a sample of the recipe to determine that it is as firm as you need.
- To test-set agar-agar, remove a spoonful of the mixture once the agar-agar has dissolved and place it in a small bowl in the fridge. If after 10 minutes it is very *soft*, you will need to add more agar-agar to your mixture. To do this, heat a small amount of water and stir in a little

agar-agar until it dissolves. Add this to your mixture and test-set once again. If the mixture is too *hard*, add a small amount of water, stock or juice to the mixture and test-set again.

FOR AGAR-AGAR BARS
- Break the bars into pieces and wash in cold water. Squeeze out the excess water and then soak 30 minutes in the liquid to be set.
- After soaking, bring the liquid to a simmer, whisking regularly until all the agar-agar has dissolved.

FOR AGAR-AGAR POWDER AND FLAKES
- These can be added to cold or simmering water, stock or juice. Whisk regularly until dissolved completely.
- Test-set.
- Pour into a pre-moistened mold or glass or ceramic dish; allow to set in the refrigerator or at room temperature.
- Turn out onto a plate to serve or cut into attractive shapes.
- agar-agar boils over easily and is messy to clean up.
- agar-agar can stick and burn so keep close while it cooks.

ARAME
This fine-cut black sea vegetable is perhaps the best place to start when introducing sea vegetables into the diet. It has a mild, slightly sweet flavor and an attractive appearance. Arame cooks quickly and it goes well in salads, pickles, vegetable dishes and sautés. Arame doubles in volume when soaked and needs to be cooked for only 5 to 15 minutes.

HIJIKI
This is a stringlike sea vegetable with strong flavor and as it requires more cooking than other sea vegetables, it is more suited to use in winter. It has a wonderful texture and its deep black color combines well with bright-colored vegetables to make attractive dishes.

Soak hijiki in plenty of water and change the soaking water twice. It will expand to as much as five times its dry volume. Discard the soaking water. Hijiki is often sautéed in oil, and if it is cooked with sweet vegetables such as onion, carrot and pumpkin, the strong fishy taste is reduced.

KOMBU
Flat, wide and green, kombu is a member of the kelp family. It contains a wealth of minerals and increases the nutritional value of all food prepared with it. Kombu can be used in

soups, casseroles, bean dishes, pickles, baking and salads. It is quite salty so it is best used in small amounts.

Use kitchen scissors to cut dry kombu or soak in warm water for 30 minutes then place on a chopping board and cut carefully (it is very slippery) with a sharp knife. Add to dried beans, legumes and grains when cooking as it makes them easier to digest.

NORI

Known as sloke in Ireland, slake in Scotland and laver in Wales, nori is one of the most easily digested sea vegetables. Nori also has one of the highest protein contents of all sea vegetables and is rich in vitamins A, B1 and niacin.

Nori aids the digestion of fried food and can be used as a condiment or wrapper or cut in strips to accompany grains, noodles and vegetables.

You can buy nori sheets in health food stores and Asian supermarkets, but the quality varies. Look for sheets with an even color and texture. Read the label to see that no additives are included. If they have been pretoasted, the sheets will be bright green; if untoasted they may be dark purple. Before using untoasted nori, toast lightly above a medium heat until the sheet is an even bright green. Use the whole sheet or cut into strips with kitchen scissors.

WAKAME

Wakame grows in deep water on long waving stems and resembles a leaf. The leaves have a mild and pleasant flavor and its bright green color adds interest to soups, salads, stews and pickles. Wakame need not be cooked but it must be soaked before using raw or in cooking. Remove the leaf from the stem. The stem is too tough for consumption but can be used to make stocks. The soaking liquid can be used for stock. Wakame has a similar nutrient value to kombu and they can be substituted for one another in recipes.

When unexpected visitors drop in at mealtimes, my cupboards speak to me with the ingredients they contain, and more often than not, this forms the inspiration for dinner.
- Make sure that food in cupboards, fridge and freezer are regularly rotated so older products are used first.
- Keep all dry stores in a cool, dark and dry environment.
- Keep oils in dark, airtight glass bottles, in the refrigerator if possible.
- Defrost your freezer as necessary.
- Try to use most frozen items within two months of freezing, though some things will keep longer.

Here is a list of ingredients I keep on hand to ensure I am always in a position to put a meal together quickly and easily.

Jars and tins almond butter, anchovies, artichoke hearts, capers, coconut milk, jams and spreads, mayonnaise, olives, pickles, tahini, tomatoes, tuna, umeboshi paste, umeboshi plums, vine leaves.

Frozen bread, fava beans, flour (various), kaffir lime leaves, pandan leaves, pastry. Stock vegetable, chicken and fish.

Dry packets Beans garbanzos (chickpeas), lima, navy (haricot), pinto, salted black. Grains couscous, oats, pearl barley, quinoa, rice (arborio and biodynamic white, brown, short grain). Starches kudzu, cornstarch. Miso gen mai, natto, shiro. Noodles green tea, rice (two varieties), soba, somen, udon. Nuts almonds, cashews, hazelnuts, pistachios, walnuts. Pasta (various). Sago. Sea vegetables agar-agar, arame, hijiki, kombu, nori. Seeds poppy, pumpkin, sesame, sunflower. Spices various.

Fresh flowers, fruit, herbs, lemons, pesto, vegetables.

Bottles green curry paste, kecap manis, laksa paste, mirin, shoyu, tamari. Oils (unrefined) extra-virgin olive, peanut, sesame, toasted sesame, virgin olive. Vinegar balsamic (aged), black, brown rice, red wine, white wine, umeboshi.

GLOSSARY OF INGREDIENTS, UTENSILS AND PREPARATION TECHNIQUES

AGAR-AGAR *see* Sea vegetables

APPLE JUICE CONCENTRATE This is a natural sweetener made by evaporating apple juice. It contains more nutrients than refined sugar and though it is not as sweet, it has a complex flavor that is well suited to use in cakes, custards and other desserts.

ARAME *see* Sea vegetables

ASHED GOAT'S CHEESE Dried goat's milk curds are formed into small log shapes or pyramids and dusted with powdered charcoal, giving them a dull, dark gray or black appearance. The rich and creamy texture complements ripe fruits in season and sourdough breads, toast or crackers.

BALSAMIC VINEGAR A red wine vinegar traditionally produced in Modena, Italy, and aged for up to 100 years. This dark brown vinegar has a unique sweet flavor and is used mostly for salad dressings, though it is delicious used sparingly over ripe fruit and added to sautéed vegetables.

BANCHA TEA TWIGS Known as kukicha in Japan. The three-year-old twigs of the green tea plant are picked and roasted. Boil a small amount of twigs in water and add more of each as needed. Will not become bitter by boiling. Bancha contains no tannin, is very low in caffeine and has a high mineral content. Hoji cha is also a bancha tea made from the leaves instead of the twigs; it has a lighter flavor and is best for drinking in summertime.

BONITO FLAKES Known as katsuo in Japan. Bonito is a fish used in a dried form. It has been dried, smoked and fermented. It keeps indefinitely and is shaved using a specialized tool. These flakes can be purchased packaged and used to make stocks and particularly dashi stock, an essential ingredient in many Japanese dishes.

BURDOCK A very long, brown root vegetable with an earthy flavor, great to use in casseroles and slow-cooked winter meals. Gobo is the Japanese name.

CAMP OVEN A deep cast-iron pot with a well-fitting lid and a handle; usually stands on short legs. Keep oiled between uses as it will rust over time if this is not done. Good for slow, even cooking over an open fire, it can be hung over the fire or placed directly on the coals.

CAROB MOLASSES A sweet syrup made by distilling carob beans in water in earthenware containers. Found in Lebanese or Middle Eastern grocery shops.

CHIEW Chinese rice wine made from glutinous rice. It is used in stocks, sauces and glazes, giving them a delicious and identifiably Chinese flavor.

COUSCOUS Wheat, usually durum wheat (a hard winter variety), that has been steamed and rolled. Couscous is eaten in North Africa with vegetable and meat stews. It is light and fluffy when cooked. It cooks fast and kids generally love it.

CUTTING STYLES
DICE this involves cutting the ingredient, usually firm vegetables and onions, into squares. Make the dice evenly sized, whether small, medium or large.

IRREGULAR CUT this suits pumpkin and other large, round vegetables. First cut into wedges, then cut at angles to get uneven but similar-sized chunks of vegetables. This cut is best suited to curries and stews.

SHAVE CUT this suits long, round vegetables such as carrots. Peel the vegetable first and then, using a sharp knife, shave the vegetable from the thin end as if you are sharpening a pencil. These pieces make good pickles and have a comfortable feel in the mouth.

WEDGE OR ROLL CUT cut carrots and similar-shaped vegetables into wedges by cutting first on the diagonal away from you, then making the next cut on the diagonal towards you, alternating like this until you have chopped the whole vegetable into wedges.

DAIKON A long, white radish which is hot when eaten raw and sweet and juicy when boiled. It also bakes well.

DEGLAZING Once you have pan-fried or roasted meat, fish or vegetables, there are valuable extracts left in the pan. To deglaze, place the pan over low heat and add liquid (stock, vinegar, verjuice or water). Stir well to lift the precious flavors from the bottom of the pan and then use as a thin sauce, or thicken for gravy. Or you might want to put it back into the dish you are making.

DRIED CHERRIES Sweet cherry varieties that have been sundried. These have an intense flavor and are a wonderful addition to desserts.

DRIED CHESTNUTS The dried fruit of the chestnut tree. They have a sweet flavor and an interesting, starchy texture that goes well with grains, vegetables and other nuts. Also very good in desserts. It must be cooked to be eaten.

EGGWASH This is made by whisking a whole egg with a little water or milk. It is painted onto baking pastry to give it a golden glaze.

FISH KETTLE These may be aluminum, enamel or stainless steel. Long and narrow, they are ideal for poaching and steaming whole fish.

GALANGAL A native of Java and Malaysia, this is a fragrant member of the ginger family. It has a camphor-like smell and is used extensively in Indonesian, Malaysian, Thai and Nonya cooking. You can buy galangal fresh, dried as powder or sliced and bottled. It has a sinuous texture when fresh and is probably easier to use bottled. Dried slices are handy for stocks but not suitable for grinding in a blender.

GEN MAI MISO *see* Miso

GHEE Clarified butter used extensively in Indian cooking.

GINGER GRATER In Japan, a small porcelain or metal grater used only for this purpose. In Indonesia, a wooden grater is kept for this purpose.

GINGER JUICE (how to make if you don't have a vegetable juicer) This is the liquid content of fresh ginger that is extracted by first grating the ginger and then squeezing it to remove juice.

GINKGO NUTS The green fruit of a female ginkgo tree. The shell is removed and the seed blanched to make it easier to peel the inner skin. Ginkgo nuts have a distinctive and unusual flavor. Used in soups and steamed custards.

GREEN CURRY PASTE This is a paste made from fresh herbs and spices and green chiles. It is well suited to Thai-style dishes and laksa. Use as much or as little as you like.

GREEN TEA

MATCHA this is very finely ground green tea used in the tea ceremony in Japan. It has a strong and bitter flavor and is best drunk hot soon after making.

SENCHA this is leaf green tea for everyday use. It is best to pour boiling water over this tea in a glass or ceramic pot and allow it to steep for a minute or two only, before straining the tea into another pot; otherwise it becomes very bitter.

HIJIKI *see* Sea vegetables

KABOCHA PUMPKIN This is the name given to a squat, dark green and golden variegated pumpkin. The flesh is dense and dark orange. It has a high starch content and a sweet flavor, making it ideal for baking and making casseroles.

KAFFIR LIMES AND LEAVES This is a distinctive Thai and East Asian ingredient. The fruit is round and has a knobbly surface that is dark green in color. The zest and juice and the leaves are added to soups, salads and curries.

It is best to add at the end of cooking, as the flavor is derived from the volatile oils contained within the skin and leaf.

KAMPYO This is the Japanese name for long strips of dried gourd. Once soaked in cold water it is used to tie ingredients into bundles and parcels for stewing. It is edible once well cooked. Also used in some types of sushi.

KETCAP MANIS (pronounced *ketchap*) This is a thick, sweet soy sauce made from soybeans and palm sugar. It is used in Indonesia to add flavor and color to dishes.

KOJI *Aspergillus oryzae* is a culture grown on brown rice. Once this is done, the rice is called koji. Once added, koji assists in the fermentation process that produces products such as miso, shoyu, amasake and rice malt.

KOMBU *see* Sea vegetables

KUDZU The ultimate thickening agent. It produces a clear smooth-textured sauce. Always dissolve it first in cold water. Used medicinally in Japan to treat minor digestive problems.

LEAVEN Also known as sourdough starter. Wheat flour and water are whisked together and left to ferment for several days to capture natural airborne yeasts and friendly bacteria. Once the leaven is active (bubbling), it is added to more flour and water to make a dough that will then rise due to the fermentation process.

LEBANESE CUCUMBERS Short thin cucumbers that have a thin edible skin and a sweet flavor. They make excellent pickles or can be used raw in salads and sandwiches.

LIGURIAN OLIVES Very small pale to dark brown olives from Liguria in Italy. The seed is relatively large but the flesh is sweet and full of flavor. They look charming and are a good addition to pasta sauces, salads and pickles.

MALTOSE SYRUP A grain sweetener made from wheat, rice or barley. It is very dense and needs to be warmed before it can be spooned from its container. Used widely in China, it is painted onto ducks before roasting and used in sauces and desserts. It is less sweet than refined sucrose but is easier for the body to digest, being a more complex sweetener.

MANDOLIN A wooden, stainless steel or plastic vegetable slicer. It comes with several metal blades for fine slicing and grating. Useful for cutting large quantities.

MILLET A small, round, yellow grain that has been a staple food in Africa and China for centuries. When cooked well, it fluffs up to approximately three times its volume. Mostly suited to autumn and winter eating. Great in soups and as a side dish.

MIRIN Mirin is a Japanese sweet rice wine, it is ideal to balance flavors in many dishes. The best-quality mirin is drunk in small amounts as an aperitif, a little like sherry.

MISO This is a fermented soybean paste which comes in many varieties. Grain is added to the fermenting beans and the texture and flavor varies depending on the grains used. The length of the fermentation process also contributes to flavor.

GEN MAI MISO a brown rice miso usually about three years old. This makes great flavored soup and condiments. Mugi miso, which is made from barley, can be substituted for gen mai.

NATTO MISO a sweet miso made with young barley and kombu and fermented for only thirty days. It is mainly used for condiments. It is not used for soups. It has a rough texture where the others are predominantly smooth.

SHIRO MISO a white miso paste made from white rice and soybeans, fermented for one year only. It is sweet miso and is ideal for sauces or mild soups.

MUSHROOMS

PORCINI a fragrant dried Italian mushroom. They have a marvelous earthy flavor that suits soups, sauces, pasta and risotto. When fresh, these mushrooms are known as cépes.

SHIITAKE MUSHROOMS (FRESH AND DRIED) fresh mushrooms should be plump and golden brown. Discard the stems before using in soups, sauces and vegetable dishes. Cook lightly to retain their delicate flavor.

Dried shiitakes need to be soaked before use and also need cooking. The best-quality specimens are thick in the center. Discard their stems before use as they are too tough to eat.

NATTO MISO *see* Miso

NOODLES These come in many varieties and are made from wheat, rice, yam or bean flour. For more details, see pages 23-26.

NORI *see* Sea vegetables

ONIONS

FRENCH SHALLOTS also known as eshalots and golden shallots. Milder than onions, French shallots are quite small, have brown skin and come with several bulbs attached to the one plant.

GREEN ONIONS also known as scallions, shallots and spring onions. These are long, green onions with an undeveloped bulb. Both the white and green part can be used in cooking.

RED ONIONS also known as Spanish onions. A colorful onion, often used in salads and salsas, they have a sweeter, milder flavor than brown onions.

SALAD ONIONS also known as spring or new onions. These are green onions with a more developed bulb than the green onion (above).

YELLOW ONIONS also known as brown onions. These have a sharp taste when raw.

ORANGE FLOWER WATER This distilled water in which orange blossoms have been soaking is very potent and is best used sparingly to flavor syrups and desserts. It is used widely in the Middle East.

PALM SUGAR Also called djaggery (India), gula malacca or gula jawa (Indonesia). This is the sap of a specific palm flower boiled to crystallize its natural sugars. It is less refined than most table sugars and contains more nutrients. It has a beautiful flavor that complements coconut and lemon and is suitable for both Asian and non-Asian dishes.

QUINOA (pronounced *keenwa*) A nutritious grain grown high in the Andes. It is most suitable used as a whole grain. It is easily and quickly cooked and has an interesting texture. Quinoa is gluten-free.

RICE FLOUR Flour made from finely milled whole-grain or white rice. It is coarser than wheat flour and does not contain gluten. Rice flour can be used to thicken dishes. It gives a crispness to biscuits when added to other flours.

RICE MALT Also known as rice syrup or yinnie syrup. This is a sweet syrup made by adding koji rice culture to brown rice and then reducing to a syrup by boiling or vacuum extraction. Used to sweeten sauces, vegetable dishes and desserts.

RICE VINEGAR Can be made from brown or white rice. When you buy an authentic bottle you will experience its special flavor. It is an excellent accompaniment to fish and makes fabulous pickles and dressings. Accept no substitute for the real thing.

ROOIBOS TEA A tea made from the small red needle-like leaf of the South African red bush. Brewed by boiling, this tea contains no tannin or caffeine. It can be simmered endlessly and will not turn bitter. It has a delicious taste that goes well with sweet spices.

SAUERKRAUT Cabbage fermented with salt and sometimes caraway and white wine. Sauerkraut made by lactic acid fermentation develops a wonderful flavor and retains all its original nutrients.

SEA VEGETABLES

AGAR-AGAR known as kanten in Japan. A clear gelatin made from sea vegetables. agar-agar is used to make jams, jellies, aspics and molds. It is a good source of calcium and iron.

ARAME fine sliced black sea vegetable. Can be used in soups, salads, condiments or pickles. Arame has a palatable mild flavor and is therefore an ideal introduction to sea vegetables.

HIJIKI a string-like sea vegetable, it has the strongest flavor of all sea vegetables. Suited to use during winter, it is ideal cooked well with sweet, brightly colored vegetables and it is quite delicious when served with sesame and soy.

KOMBU also known as konbu, kelp or seatangle. Kombu is flat, wide and green. It has a high mineral content and increases the nutritional value of all food prepared with it.

It is used for stocks, soups, casseroles, bean dishes, pickles, baking and salads. It has quite a high salt content and is therefore best used in small amounts.

NORI also known as laver. This is a marine algae made into very thin sheets and sold either dried when it is purple in color, or toasted when it becomes bright green. It is important to store it in an airtight container. Use it crushed as a condiment, or to wrap rice as sushi. It can also be bought in small flakes to add to grain and vegetable dishes.

WAKAME a mild-flavored sea vegetable that grows in deep waters. The leaf is used in soups, stocks, salads, stews and pickles. It has a high calcium content and is also rich in niacin and thiamine. Pre-prepared flakes may be bought packaged in small quantities. All you need to do is add a pinch to water.

SHIRO MISO *see* Miso

SHOYU A light thin soy sauce produced from fermented soybeans, wheat and salt. It also comes salt-reduced. My advice is to buy regular and use less of it.

SLAPPAP POT Slappap is Afrikaans for soft porridge. The pot traditionally used to make this is a large cast-iron camp oven with three legs.

SUCANAT This is dried sugarcane juice with nothing added or extracted. It therefore contains all the nutritional value of the plant, unlike refined sugarcane. It can be used in exactly the same way as refined sugar, but it does add color to dishes.

SUGAR SNAP PEAS This member of the pea family is a sweet and tender variety that is eaten in its entirety, pod and all. The pods are bright green and need little cooking. Use them in soups, stirfries and salads or steam a handful, add a little salt and olive oil and feast on these as an entrée.

TAHINI, HULLED This is made by grinding hulled sesame seeds to a paste. It is used in the Middle East and Japan to make sauces, as a spread and in savory dishes and desserts. Tahini has a high calcium content and as the hulls contain large amounts of oxalic acid, the hulled variety is preferable.

TAMARI A thick soy sauce made without wheat. A traditional Japanese product, originally a by-product from miso production.

TEMPEH A traditional Indonesian food made when soybeans are exposed to a mold (*Rhizopus oligosporus*) which is much like the white mold found on Camembert cheese. Sliced thinly and fried crisp, tempeh can be a great substitute for bacon. I like it fried first and then cooked with Asian flavors. It is a good source of protein, quite delicious in curries and dips, and also marinated and grilled.

TOASTED SESAME OIL Oil extracted from toasted sesame seeds. This is a dark oil with a pervasive flavor. It is best used in very small amounts towards the end of cooking. Not suitable to fry or sauté with.

TOFU POCKETS Known as abura age in Japan. Deep-fried tofu skins cut in half and opened carefully to create a pocket that can then be marinated and filled with noodles and vegetables or with a rice filling. The pockets can then be simmered in stock or eaten cold. Torn pockets can be finely sliced and added to soups and broths.

TRIVET This is a loose steamer that fits inside the fish kettle. It has a handle at either end that allows easy access to the whole fish going in and coming out of the kettle.

UMEBOSHI PASTE Puréed plums with the pits removed. A cheaper way to buy umeboshi if you do not require the seeds.

UMEBOSHI PLUMS Known as pickled plums, these are in fact apricots. A small green apricot pickled with salt and red shiso leaves that turn the apricots pink and give them a distinctive flavor, produced in Japan. Umeboshi plums are very salty, so use sparingly.

UMEBOSHI VINEGAR Traditionally a by-product of plum production, this is not a true vinegar and can be used by people who want to avoid fermented products. It is high in salt with a lemonlike effect. It is great in salad dressings and when a dish requires a little lift.

VERJUICE or **VERJUS** Verjuice, the juice of unripe grapes, was used extensively in the Middle Ages. It is unfermented, with a subtle flavor of grapes. Use it as an alternative to vinegar, although its taste is not as strong. Verjuice is excellent for deglazing baked fowl and vegetable dishes.

VINEGARS, BLACK AND RED Chinese rice vinegars that are excellent with steamed dumplings and in sauces to accompany fried foods. Found in Chinese and Asian supermarkets.

WAKAME *see* Sea vegetables

WASABI Also known as Japanese horseradish. This is usually bought as a green powder in small tins or as a ready-made paste. It is very strong and can cause severe pain to the sinuses if too much is eaten at once. Add very small amounts to sushi or sashimi or better still, dissolve the paste in tamari and dip the sushi or sashimi in the sauce.

WHOLE MILK This milk has had minimal treatment and still contains its full fat content. Unhomogenized milk has a layer of fat on the surface and homogenized milk does not. The vitamins that milk contains (A, D, E and K) are fat-soluble. The flavor of whole milk is so superior to regular commercial milk that you may never use anything else.

WILD RICE High in nutrients, this is a grass seed. It was the principal food of North American Indians, traditionally collected by canoe as it grew wild in lakes and river marshes.

This section of the book contains the how-to's and details about some less well-known ingredients and techniques.

When you are reading the recipes they will refer you back to these pages for details that will help you to make the dish and give you some information about selected ingredients.

STOCKS

If you buy organic produce and have the time, make your own stock. Using everything you've bought – fish heads, bones, vegetables – you can make delicious, deeply flavored stocks.

Making stock is simple. They store well and they add flavor, depth and character as well as nutritional value to dishes. Complex flavor is the aim of good cooking. Grain, noodle and vegetable dishes cooked in water will lack the complexity and interest that stocks can provide them.

It is possible to make stock from the off-cuts of vegetables, fish and chicken. However, not all off-cuts are desirable for stock, and the quality of the produce you use will determine the end result.

MAKING STOCK

Use vegetables that contribute clean, strong flavors, but are not so strong that they dominate other flavors. You also need vegetables that do not collapse completely while being boiled. The best vegetables for stock are carrots, leeks, onions, parsley stalks, celery (the leaves are not used as they are very strong and make stock cloudy), celeriac and sweet corn.

Not recommended are members of the *Brassica* family. These include cabbages, sprouts, broccoli and cauliflower. Their flavors dominate and they do not lend themselves to long cooking. Turnips and parsnips have strong flavors and also are not recommended.

- Wash all produce and ensure all items to be used are free from mold and are not rotting. Remember that although making stock is a good way to clean out the leftover vegetables from the fridge, those that are well past their prime will not add anything you want to the meal.
- Add herbs and spices to give the stock a particular character.
- If making a chicken stock, clean the cavity of a chicken thoroughly, removing any bits of gut or offal that may be present and wash well under cold running water before boiling, otherwise the stock may be bitter.
- When making fish stock, cook for approximately 20 minutes only; otherwise the stock may become gluey and unpleasant.
- When making a familiar recipe, try using a different stock as the base. You may be surprised how much difference it can make.

VEGETABLE STOCK
makes 20 cups (5 L)

2 onions, peeled and cut in half
2 large carrots, roughly chopped
1 cob sweet corn, broken in two
$\frac{1}{2}$ head celery, leaves removed, roughly chopped
1 leek, washed and roughly chopped
$\frac{3}{4}$-in (2-cm) fresh ginger, sliced
$2\frac{1}{2}$-in (6-cm) stick kombu
$5\frac{1}{2}$ quarts (22 cups/5.5 L) cold water

place all the ingredients in a large pan
bring to a simmer and cook 20 to 30 minutes
strain through a fine sieve or cheesecloth
remove the kombu to use again
discard the solids
use what you need and freeze the remainder in 4-cup (1-L) portions
note: simmer gently if you want a clear stock

FISH STOCK
makes 20 cups (5 L)

2 large fish heads or 1 whole fish or 10 prawn heads
1 bunch cilantro (coriander)
1 bunch parsley
2 large onions, roughly chopped
3 cloves garlic, roughly chopped
3 tablespoons fish sauce
1 tablespoon umeboshi vinegar
$2\frac{1}{2}$-in (6-cm) stick kombu
6 quarts (24 cups/6 L) cold water

make sure the fish is very fresh; it should smell pleasant
combine all the ingredients in a large pan
bring to a boil
skim off any scum and turn the heat down

simmer, uncovered, for 20 minutes

strain through a fine sieve and discard all the solids

cool in the refrigerator

remove any fat that rises to the surface

use what you need and freeze the remainder in 4-cup (1-L) portions

JAPANESE VEGETABLE STOCK
dashi #1 makes 12 cups (3 L)

6-in (15-cm) stick kombu, washed and cut into 3-in (7.5-cm) strips

3 dried shiitake mushrooms

2 large carrots, roughly chopped

1 leek, washed and roughly chopped

12 cups (3 L) water

place the kombu, mushrooms, carrots and leek in a pan with the water

bring slowly to a simmer

simmer for 30 minutes

strain through a fine sieve

keep the kombu and mushrooms to use in another dish

discard the vegetables

use what you need of the stock and freeze the remainder in 4-cup (1-L) portions

JAPANESE FISH STOCK
dashi #2 makes 12 cups (3 L)

12 cups (3 L) water

4-in (10-cm) stick kombu, washed and cut with scissors

3 tablespoons bonito flakes (shaved dried fish)

fill pan with water and add kombu

slowly bring to a simmer

simmer for 10 minutes

add the bonito flakes and simmer for a further 5 minutes

strain through a fine sieve

use what you need of the stock and freeze the remainder in 4-cup (1-L) portions

note: this stock can be made stronger by simmering the kombu and bonito longer

ASIAN VEGETABLE STOCK
makes 20 cups (5 L)

2 onions, peeled and cut in half
2 large carrots, roughly chopped
1/2 head celery, leaves removed, roughly chopped
1 leek, washed and roughly chopped
2-in (5-cm) fresh ginger, sliced
1 bunch cilantro (coriander) stems, washed well
4 kaffir lime leaves
2 sticks lemongrass (bash the thick ends to release the full flavor)
5 quarts (20 cups/5 L) cold water

place all the ingredients in a large pan
bring to a simmer and cook 20 to 30 minutes
skim off the scum that rises to the surface
strain through a fine sieve or cheesecloth
discard the solids
use what you need of the stock and freeze the remainder in 4-cup (1-L) portions
note: simmer gently if you want a clear stock

BASIC CHICKEN STOCK
makes 20 cups (5 L)

1 whole boiling chicken or a chicken carcass
2 onions, cut into large chunks
3 large carrots, cut into large chunks
1 leek, washed and cut into large chunks
1/2 celeriac root, peeled and diced or 1/2 head celery, leaves removed, cut into medium chunks
1 bunch parsley
1 bunch of a herb of your choosing
6 quarts (24 cups/6 L) cold water
4 1/2 teaspoons sea salt
4 1/2 teaspoons fish sauce or 3 1/2 teaspoons umeboshi vinegar

remove any remaining innards from the chicken, especially any pockets of offal that have been left behind; they can make a stock bitter

wash chicken under cold water

place all the ingredients in a large pan

bring to a boil

turn the heat down and simmer gently for 1½ hours (reduce further for a stronger stock)

do not allow to boil vigorously

strain the stock and cool in the refrigerator

remove the fat from the surface once cold

freeze any stock you will not use within two days

GAME BIRD STOCK

makes 12 cups (3 L)

1 pheasant or duck or chicken carcass
½ leek, washed and roughly chopped
1 carrot, roughly chopped
1 onion, cut into medium dice
2 sticks celery, cut into medium dice
11 cups (2.75 L) water

place the bird carcass in a baking dish

place in the oven at 335°F (170°C) for 30 minutes to brown

if you are making duck stock:

remove the baking dish from the oven every 15 minutes and pour the fat into a ceramic bowl

put the duck fat in the fridge to solidify

keep this fat to fry potatoes in or to confit duck legs in the future or freeze if you wish

remove the browned carcass to a large saucepan

deglaze the baking dish with 1 cup (8 fl oz/250 ml) verjuice or water, add this to the stock pot

add all the vegetables and 11 cups (2.75 L) water to the stock pot

bring to a boil and cook, uncovered, for 2 to 3 hours, adding more water as needed

strain stock and discard the bones and vegetables

allow to cool completely in the fridge

remove any fat that has solidified on the surface of the stock

use the stock now or portion and freeze for later use

WHOLE GRAINS

Grains are inexpensive, nourishing and satisfying. They go well with almost everything.

   Full of complex carbohydrates, grains release sugars and nutrients slowly into the system, unlike simple sugars. If you're not used to eating grains, start with small amounts; prepare them according to the recipes and chew them well.

COOKING GRAINS

Properly cooked grains make a delightful component of a meal – if not well cooked they can be dull and hard work to eat and digest.

- Sort before cooking and remove any stones or debris.
- Wash to remove dirt and husks that may have lingered.
- Add sea salt at the beginning of cooking, as this helps the grain to fully absorb the liquid and contributes to a sweeter, full flavor.
- Use a pan with a tight-fitting lid. Do not disturb during cooking unless instructed.
- To dry-roast grains, stir continuously over medium heat, add boiling water or stock once the grains are golden and nutty smelling. Be careful of the steam created.

See if you can develop a nose for cooked grain. It takes practice but it can be done. You can also develop an ear – the cooking sound changes once all the liquid is absorbed.

BARLEY

Available as whole barley, or polished to pearl barley. Barley water, made from pearl barley, is a thirst-relieving drink and barley is also an important ingredient in liquor and beer production. In Japan it is roasted to make a cold or hot tea in summer and also in the production of mugi miso and natto miso. To cook, use 1 cup barley to 4 to 5 cups water or stock.

BUCKWHEAT

A variety of bistort grass, buckwheat is high in protein and minerals. Whole buckwheat makes a quick and nourishing winter meal, especially if the grain is dry-roasted before the liquid is added. It does not tolerate overcooking. To cook, use 1 cup buckwheat to $2\frac{1}{2}$ cups water. Buckwheat flour is excellent for pancakes and blinis and is used to make soba noodles in Japan.

SWEET CORN/MAIZE

This versatile grain can be eaten fresh, or dried and ground, crushed or rolled. It comes in a variety of colors: white, blue, black, red and most commonly, a deep yellow.

Sweet corn is very sweet when fresh but as it ages the sugar in the kernels turns to starch and the sweet flavor is lost. It is best to eat fresh corn as close to picking as possible.

MILLET

A small round, yellow seedlike grain, providing vitamin B, iron, phosphorus and lecithin. Millet has a higher protein content than corn, oats or rice.

I like it best when it has been evenly dry-roasted or cooked in a little oil before the water is added. This gives it a nutty flavor, and ensures all the grains pop open.

Millet makes a good winter porridge and goes well with cooked fruit for breakfast. I sometimes use millet flour as an alternative to wheat flour in pancakes with good results.

Add boiling water or stock to millet, being careful of the steam that is created if the grain is hot from dry-roasting. To cook, use 1 cup millet to 3 cups water or stock.

OATS

Oats are available as whole groats, crushed, cut or rolled. They are a good source of protein and contain vitamin B1 and a number of unsaturated fatty acids. Ground oats make a wonderful addition to biscuits, and oat milk is a good dairy milk substitute.

WHEAT

Wheat has become an extremely important grain worldwide. It is, however, associated with allergies. Some people are allergic only to the processed flour products and do not have problems digesting cooked, presoaked, whole-wheat berries, sprouted wheat or wheat germ.

The high gluten content of wheat makes it perfect for bread baking. Soft wheat suits cakes and biscuits and hard winter or durum wheat is ideal for making seitan, couscous, semolina and pasta. To cook, use 1 cup wheat berries to 3 cups water or stock.

RICE

Rice is a staple in many countries. It is easy to digest and free of gluten. It is a nourishing grain. The nutritional value is greater when the rice is unpolished (brown), but throughout Asia the preference is for white rice.

Rice is high in starch, and digestion is aided by chewing thoroughly. If chewing is impaired, cook the rice with more liquid and for longer so that it is softer and easier to digest. Made as a thin gruel and cooked with medicinal ingredients ("congee"), rice is used to heal sickness of all sorts.

Australia produces excellent short- and long-grain biodynamically grown rice. It costs more but it still makes an inexpensive meal and is worth it for both nutrition and flavor.

There are three distinct groups of rice:
- Round or short-grain rice from the Japonica family. These grains cling when cooked and are more easily eaten with chopsticks. Japonica family includes short brown rice, short white rice and arborio rice.
- Long-grain rice from the Indica family cooks so the grains are separate and it does not have a sticky character. Included in the Indica family are Thai jasmine rice, patna and basmati rice.

- Long- and short-grain rice of the Javinica family. These are the sticky or glutinous rices such as black and white sticky rice, and are used mainly for desserts, except in the north of Thailand, Cambodia, Laos and parts of Vietnam, where long-grain sticky white rice is the staple.

RICE VARIETIES AND DISHES

In cultures where rice is a staple, fine distinctions are made about the many varieties, and people are particular about which variety suits which dish. In Asia it is most important to use the correct grain for a dish.

For Chinese and Japanese dishes and some Vietnamese dishes to be eaten with chopsticks, use rice that clings. Japonica family, short-grain rice.

For Thai-style dishes, use jasmine rice. As the name implies, it is scented with jasmine flavor. Indica family, long-grain rice.

For Indian, Malaysian and Sri Lankan dishes, use basmati and patna rice, as these varieties will cook as separate grains. For a really fluffy dish use the pilau method (page 52) that cooks the raw grains in oil or ghee to coat them first before adding boiling stock. Indica family, long-grain rice.

For Filipino and Indonesian meals, grains should be cooked somewhere between fluffy and clinging. Use Japonica family with a little less liquid, or roast first, then add boiling stock.

For risotto and paellas, use arborio (for risotto) and calasperra (for paella) to get the best results. These varieties are short and absorb a large amount of liquid. They can also be used for rice puddings with good results. Japonica family.

There are as many ideas about the correct method of cooking rice as there are people that eat it. These are the methods I use.

BASIC: THE ABSORPTION METHOD

This is really a steaming technique and the rice has to stand for some time after the liquid has been absorbed so the steam can continue to soften the grains. If you are using stock instead of water, take into account any salt the stock contains so you are not adding salt twice. Remember when cooking large amounts of rice that you need to reduce the ratio of water to grain slightly. The ratios given are suitable for up to 3 lb (1.5 kg) rice.

1 cup ($6^{1}/_{2}$ oz/200 g) short-grain brown rice to 2 cups (16 fl oz/500 ml) water or stock
$^{1}/_{2}$ teaspoon sea salt per cup of rice

wash rice well; drain

place rice in pan; cover with liquid and add sea salt

cover pan with a tight-fitting lid

place over high heat and bring rapidly to a boil

listen for the pot to boil and watch for steam rather than remove the lid

reduce the heat so rice is just simmering

cook approximately 45 minutes or until all the liquid has been absorbed

remove the lid and gently turn the grains over using a flat wooden spoon

replace lid for 5 minutes before serving

PRESSURE COOKING SHORT-GRAIN BROWN RICE

1 cup (6$\frac{1}{2}$oz/200g) rice to 1$\frac{1}{2}$ cups (12floz/375ml) water or stock

$\frac{1}{2}$ teaspoon sea salt per cup of rice

wash rice well and drain

place rice in the pressure cooker; cover with liquid and add sea salt

cover with the lid

place on full heat to bring rapidly to a boil

allow to rise to full pressure

reduce the heat so rice is just simmering

cook for approximately 35 minutes

turn off the heat and allow the pressure to drop

remove the lid and gently turn the grains over using a flat wooden spoon

note: pressure cooked rice has a lovely, slightly sticky texture and is easier to digest than boiled rice; best in autumn and winter

LONG-GRAIN BROWN RICE

Boiling: 1 cup (6$\frac{1}{2}$oz/200g) rice to 1$\frac{1}{2}$ cups (12floz/375ml) liquid for 30 minutes

Pressure cooking: 1 cup (6$\frac{1}{2}$oz/200g) rice to 1$\frac{1}{4}$ cups (10floz/310ml) water or stock for 25 minutes

BROWN BASMATI RICE

Carefully remove any small stones from the grain. Basmati rice always seems to be dirtier than the rest. Wash well until the water runs clear.

Boiling: 1 cup (6$\frac{1}{2}$oz/200g) rice to 1$\frac{1}{2}$ cups (12floz/375ml) liquid for 20 minutes

As basmati cooks quickly and I mostly eat it in summer, I do not pressure cook it. It is wonderful cooked in the pilau way.

PILAU RICE
serves 5

2 tablespoons light olive oil or ghee
1 onion, finely diced
2 cups (12 oz/400 g) basmati rice, cleaned, washed and drained well, and left 30 minutes to dry
2 green cardamom pods, bruised
1 whole clove
1 stick cinnamon
4 cups (1 L) stock
1$\frac{1}{2}$ teaspoons sea salt
a few saffron threads (optional)

heat a heavy pan that has a well-fitting lid
add the oil or ghee
sauté the onion until it is golden brown
pour in the rice and add the spices
stir gently to coat each grain with oil or ghee
sauté for 3 minutes, stirring gently
in a separate pan bring the stock and sea salt to a simmer
add the simmering stock to the rice and cover immediately with the lid
turn the heat to low and cook for 20 minutes
turn off the flame and leave, covered, for 5 minutes
uncover and leave 5 minutes more to allow the steam to escape
fluff with a metal fork to prevent breaking the grains

THAI JASMINE RICE
1 cup (6$\frac{1}{2}$ oz/200 g) rice to 1$\frac{1}{2}$ cups (12 fl oz/375 ml) water or stock
1 pinch salt per cup rice

boil rice for 20 minutes

RED RICE
1 cup (6$\frac{1}{2}$ oz/200 g) rice to 1$\frac{3}{4}$ cups (14 fl oz/450 ml) water or stock

boil rice for 40 minutes

SWEET GLUTINOUS WHITE RICE OR BLACK RICE PUDDING
serves 4

1 1/4 cups (8 oz/250 g) long-grain glutinous rice
3/4 cup plus 2 tablespoons (7 fl oz/200 ml) coconut milk
1/4 teaspoon sea salt

TOPPING
freshly grated coconut
1 tablespoon grated palm sugar
ripe sugar bananas

wash the rice and cover with cold water
leave to soak for 6 to 8 hours or overnight, then drain well
place rice, coconut milk and salt in a heatproof dish and stir well
place dish over boiling water, cover and steam for 1 hour
or pressure cook in a heatproof dish at half-pressure for 30 minutes
remove mixture from pan when cooled slightly
using damp hands, form the rice into pyramid shapes
serve with a little coconut, palm sugar and slices of banana
use the day it is made; it tends to dry out if refrigerated

WILD RICE
serves 4

1 cup (5 1/2 oz/160 g) wild rice
4 cups (1 L) water
1/2 teaspoon sea salt

place rice, water and salt in a pan
cover and bring to a boil
turn the heat to low and simmer for 45 minutes
fluff up the grains with a fork
drain any remaining liquid and reserve to use as stock

RICE CONGEE

This is an excellent soup when you are feeling cold, weak and generally unwell. A crockpot works very well for this and you can cook it all day if you choose. Add more water rather than less.

You can add other ingredients as you wish. Fish and chicken stock make good congee too.

2 handfuls short-grain brown or white rice
4 cups (1 L) water or stock
1 teaspoon sea salt
3 green onions (scallions), finely chopped
$\frac{1}{4}$ teaspoon toasted sesame oil per serving
2 tablespoons finely sliced ginger

combine the rice, water or stock, and sea salt in a large pan
bring to a simmer
turn the flame as low as possible and place the pan on a diffuser
cook for 4 hours
serve in deep bowls topped with some green onions, sesame oil and slices of ginger

ROASTED TOMATOES

These tomatoes are very handy to have on hand for a fast pasta-based or grain-based dish.

1 lb (500 g) cherry or roma tomatoes, washed and dried
$\frac{1}{2}$ teaspoon sea salt
freshly ground black pepper to taste
3 tablespoons olive oil
2 sticks rosemary
6 sage leaves

combine all the ingredients on a baking tray
place in the oven at 400°F (200°C) for 35 minutes
serve immediately or cool and store in an airtight container in the fridge until needed

ROASTING NUTS AND SEEDS

WHEN OVEN-ROASTING NUTS AND SEEDS

- Check before you begin that the nuts or seeds are fresh. Stale nuts will ruin your dishes.
- Shell nuts and seeds before roasting.
- Preheat the oven to 325°F (160°C). It is better to roast for longer at a low temperature as nuts and seeds have a high oil content and burn easily.

- Spread the nuts or seeds evenly on a baking sheet, discarding blackened or rotten ones.
- Place in the middle of the oven and check after 10 minutes to see how they are going. Shuffle them about so they will roast evenly.
- Remove from the oven when they are golden brown.
- Cool completely before using or storing.
- Store in an airtight container and use within a week for best flavor and texture.
- Roast different types of nuts and seeds on separate sheets.

WHEN PAN-ROASTING NUTS AND SEEDS
- As above, check that nuts and seeds are fresh.
- If the seeds you are using are dusty, first wash and drain them well in a fine sieve.
- Heat a heavy frying pan on medium heat.
- Pour in the nuts or seeds and stir them with a wooden spoon to ensure they cook evenly.
- When the aroma changes and they begin to pop and turn golden brown, they are ready.
- Remove from the pan immediately as it retains the heat and they will continue to cook.
- Place on a plate or tray to cool.
- Cool completely before serving or storing.
- Store in an airtight container and use within a week.

Nuts and seeds are best roasted as you need them. If you add hot nuts to a dish they are likely to lose some of their crisp texture. Nuts and seeds add color and texture to dishes, provide protein and minerals and make attractive, nutritious snacks.

FLAVORED TAMARIS
I find these flavored tamaris add interest to Asian dishes and they are simple to make.

MANDARIN TAMARI
1 organic mandarin orange skin, dried in the sun or on a heater for about 12 hours
1 cup (8 fl oz/250 ml) tamari

break the mandarin skin into pieces and put them into a bottle or glass jar with a well-fitting lid
pour in the tamari and leave for 1 month before using
top up the bottle with tamari as you use it and replace the mandarin next season
This will keep indefinitely if the mandarin skin is completely dry when it goes in.

STAR ANISE TAMARI
4 points star anise
1 cup (8 fl oz/250 ml) tamari

place the points of star anise in a glass bottle or jar with a well-fitting lid
pour in the tamari and leave for 1 month before using
top up the jar with tamari as you use it and replace the star anise once a year
This keeps indefinitely and gets stronger as it ages.

KUDZU

Kudzu is the starch from a tap root that grows in the mountains of northern Japan. It can be used to thicken any sauce, stew or casserole. It is said to have soothing properties and to be beneficial to the stomach and intestines. Used for drinks and gruels and to help stop a running nose, headache, nausea or genral tiredness. It is rather an expensive ingredient and cornstarch (cornflour) can be used instead when it's used as a thickener. However, kudzu is a superior thickening agent.

   When using kudzu follow these steps for lump-free thickening:
- Measure the kudzu and place it in a bowl.
- Add enough cold water so that the kudzu is suspended in it.
- Use your fingers to ensure that there are no lumps in the mixture.
- Do not stir yet as the kudzu settles quickly to the bottom of the bowl.
- Have the sauce that you wish to thicken at a simmer.
- Take the sauce off the heat before adding the kudzu mixture.
- Stir the kudzu mixture just before adding to the sauce.
- Pour in the kudzu mixture, stirring the sauce as you do so.
- The sauce will look cloudy at this stage.
- Continue to stir over low heat until the mixture is smooth and thickened.

MISO

Miso is a fermented soybean paste made by combining cooked soybeans, a grain, sea salt and koji (*Aspergillus oryzae* culture grown on rice). These are mixed well and left to ferment for one month to several years. The color of the miso reflects the grain mixed with it and the length of time it is left to ferment. The flavors vary accordingly from sweet to very salty.

   Generally the type of miso used corresponds to climate. There are many varieties of miso. The pale, less fermented misos are suited to warm climates. The red and moderately fermented misos are suited to temperate regions. The dark misos that have undergone long fermentation are suited to cold climates when hard work is required.

   The ones I use most often living in Sydney are
- Sweet white rice (shiro) miso for sauces and soups
- Brown rice (gen mai) miso for everyday uses

- Barley (natto) miso as a condiment and as an addition to summer dishes. This miso is made with barley, barley malt, sea salt, ginger and finely shredded kombu. Fermented for only one month, it is sweet with a coarse texture, suitable for sauces and stirfries.

Unpasteurized organic miso contains active lactobacillus, a bacteria beneficial to digestion, also found in yogurt and sauerkraut which is killed by prolonged cooking at high temperatures. Miso may also contain traces of vitamin B12.

LEGUMES: BEANS, PEAS AND LENTILS

Combined with vegetables and grains, beans provide protein, digestible fats, carbohydrates, several of the B group vitamins, calcium, iron and potassium. When beans and peas are sprouted they also provide vitamin C and a variety of enzymes.

If you are not used to eating beans regularly:
- Eat small amounts at a time and chew them very well.
- Do not feed beans to children under two as they have not yet fully developed the enzymes within their intestines that assist in the digestion of beans.
- Adding salt to beans at the beginning of cooking prevents them from softening.

COOKING LEGUMES

measure the amount of beans required

pour them into a bowl or pan and pick out any stones or discolored beans

rinse well under cold running water

cover with water to 2 in (5 cm) and soak for 4 to 12 hours

soaking speeds up the cooking time and softens the skins

discard the soaking water – it's where the gas-producing enzymes are released

place in a pan and cover with fresh cold water

bring to a boil, uncovered, then simmer

strain off any scum or foam that rises to the surface

once the beans have stopped producing scum, add a strip of kombu sea vegetable which will add minerals and flavor and assists in softening the beans

continue to simmer until all beans are softened

keep covered with water during the entire cooking time

strain the beans

season the beans once they are cooked

Do not leave out of the fridge for long, as beans ferment easily, before and after cooking.

BREAD

Leaven

I have risen in the night when it was dark and warm around me. I am standing now quite tall with a dome I know will please you; I have the knowledge of several thousand years behind me; I am grown from air and the earth's sweet blessings. It is my duty to feed you and your delight. Warm the fire beneath me now and wait while I grow crusty and divine, a golden font of memories. I will meet you in an hour — give me constant reassurance with temperature and air and I will give you sustenance and connect you to your roots. I am bread, not from a plastic wrapper or bought at your local store. I am the bread your ancestors baked, a heavier relation, the one so often forgotten. My food is not the quickening rise of commercial yeasts and sugars but the delicate bloom upon the grains of healthy wheat.

Star anise and almond steamed sourdough buns

BREAD

Good-quality bread, chewed thoroughly, provides us with complex flavors and excellent texture and acts as a vehicle for many accompaniments. Most cultures have at some time in their development used ground grain to produce a form of bread. Some were unleavened crusty flat loaves, some were made with a leaven to lighten the loaf.

Whole-wheat grains, if closely examined, have a "bloom" on them, similar to the bloom on grapes. It is a dull coating that is removed if rubbed by hand. It is this bloom that carries the spores of yeast that are activated when the grain is ground. The bloom combines with the inner starch, and by adding water, warmth and time, lactic acid fermentation occurs, creating a sour flavor. The mixture is seen to bubble and rise, and this natural leaven assists in the digestion of wheat, providing a nourishing loaf of bread.

In autumn and winter I bake bread, large loaves that warm the house, and evoke fond memories of my youth with their comforting smell.

In spring I am more inclined to steam bread and buns and make flat breads. These involve less time in the kitchen and are generally easier to digest.

I am often told kneading is hard work, but it need not be. I find it a useful meditation. I stand on a block of wood to raise myself so I can effortlessly push down the dough using my body's weight. I pull the dough from the back of the bowl to the center of the dough ball and push down and slightly away from my body. I turn the bowl a quarter turn to the left and repeat the action until the dough is smooth and stretchy. The texture of the dough, when the kneading is complete, will resemble the feel of an earlobe gently squeezed.

LEAVEN

Makes 11 cups (2.75 L)

4 cups (1 lb 3 oz/600 g) whole-wheat flour
6 cups (1.5 L) filtered water

whisk 2 cups (9½ oz/300 g) flour and 3 cups (24 fl oz/750 ml) water to a smooth batter in a bowl
cover with a clean cloth and leave to stand 1 to 3 days
whisk the mixture twice each day
when the mixture is bubbling, whisk in the remaining flour and water
repeat the daily care until the mixture again forms bubbles
now it is ready to use
keep leaven in a screw-top jar in the refrigerator

FOR CARE OF YOUR LEAVEN

Leaven can be kept active for years. Some are said to be hundreds, if not thousands, of years old. Leavens may be damaged or killed by excess heat, too much sea salt, poor-quality tap water, and by the introduction of other food particles or chemicals such as detergent.

To maintain your leaven keep a small amount aside when baking. Whisk in 1 cup (5 oz/150 g) flour and 1½ cups (12 fl oz/375 ml) spring or filtered water before returning the leaven to the refrigerator. Do this once a month if the leaven remains unused.

If you forget to keep some leaven aside you can mix a piece of dough you have made with more flour and water.

When wishing to bake again, take the leaven and pour into a clean ceramic or glass bowl, add a little of the flour you will be baking with and some water and whisk well. Set aside under a clean dish towel for approximately 1 hour, less time is needed in hot weather.

Use what you need but retain at least ½ cup (4 fl oz/ 125 ml) leaven for future use.

If unattended for a long time, leaven will become very sour and may have a layer of dark liquid on the top. Carefully remove this layer, take a teaspoon of the leaven and discard the remainder. Add fresh flour and water and whisk well. Leave covered until bubbly then treat as before.

CRUSTY SESAME SOURDOUGH LOAF

John Downes, the baker, insists sourdough breads should be left at least 12 hours before being eaten, but who do you know that can delay gratification so long?

Makes 1 (1½ lb/750 g) loaf
Season: autumn/winter

3⅓ cups (1 lb/500 g) whole-wheat flour
3½ oz (100 g) sesame seeds, lightly toasted
2 teaspoons sea salt
1 cup (8 fl oz/250 ml) filtered water
1 cup (8 fl oz/250 ml) leaven (page 63)
olive oil

combine the flour and seeds in a large clean bowl
mix the salt and water together to ensure even distribution
pour the leaven into the flour and mix with your hands
knead the mix, slowly adding the saltwater
when a ball has formed, turn onto a floured board
continue to knead to the texture of an earlobe when squeezed
rest the dough and your arms for 10 minutes
brush a heavy 2-lb (1-kg) bread pan with the olive oil
roll the dough out to the length of the pan
place the dough with seam side down in the pan
oil the top of the loaf
leave to rise, covered with a damp cloth, for 4 to 8 hours (the warmer the spot, the faster the rise and the stronger the flavor)
slow rising in a cool spot produces a sweeter loaf
preheat the oven to 400°F (200°C)
put the uncovered pan in the middle of the oven
bake for approximately 45 minutes (the loaf should look golden and sound hollow when the base is tapped)
allow to cool on a wire rack

STAR ANISE AND ALMOND STEAMED SOURDOUGH BUNS

Makes 16 buns
Season: spring/summer

one recipe sesame sourdough bread dough (page 64), omitting the sesame seeds

FILLING
7½ teaspoons corn oil
3 cloves garlic, finely chopped
2½ inches fresh ginger, very finely sliced
1 bunch bok choy, white part cut into ¼-in (0.5-cm) pieces, leaves cut into ½-in (1-cm) pieces, keep white and green parts separate
8 oz (250 g) fresh or canned water chestnuts, roughly chopped (peel if fresh)
2 tablespoons star anise tamari (page 55)
2 tablespoons ketcap manis
2 heaping teaspoons kudzu or cornstarch (cornflour), mixed with 2 tablespoons cold water
4 oz (125 g) dry-roasted almonds, roughly chopped

roll the dough into a long log, and cut into 16 even pieces
set these aside on a floured board covered with a damp cloth
heat a heavy frying pan
add the oil and sauté the garlic and ginger for 2 minutes
stir in the white of the bok choy with the water chestnuts
cook 3 minutes
add the bok choy leaves
stir in the tamari and ketcap manis; cook 3 minutes
the mixture will release liquid at this point
stir in the kudzu or cornstarch slurry
toss in the almonds, stir and set aside to cool a little
pull one piece of dough at a time into a circle 1½ in (4 cm) in diameter
place one-sixteenth of the filling in the center
pull up the edges of dough to join above the center and twist to close
pinch off any excess dough
sit the buns on a small square of parchment paper inside a bamboo or metal steamer
leave ¼ in (0.5 cm) between each one to allow them to rise
cover with a damp cloth and leave to rise until kissing each other
cover the steamer and place over a pot of cold water
slowly bring to a boil
steam for 15 minutes
spray the buns with a fine mist of water (this creates a glaze)
continue to steam for 5 more minutes

MARK WARREN'S UNDERGROUND DAMPER

Mark was one of Manna's first and most loyal customers. He is a talented potter, and some may recall the crockery he made for Iku's opening. Mark lives in northern New South Wales, where I have had the pleasure of sharing this loaf with him on several grand occasions.

Be sure if you make this bread that the ground you dig up is not precious to anyone!

Serves 6 to 8
Season: all

3½ cups (1 lb 3 oz/600 g) freshly ground whole-wheat flour plus some for kneading
1 oz (30 g) sesame seeds
2 teaspoons (½ oz/15 g) sea salt
1 cup (8 fl oz/250 ml) filtered water
1 cup (8 fl oz/250 ml) leaven (page 63)

follow the recipe for crusty sesame sourdough loaf on page 64
oil a camp oven
place the dough in it and allow it to rise, covered with a clean damp cloth, for 6 to 8 hours or overnight
dig a hole to the depth of the camp oven
build a fire with hardwood until there are enough embers to line the hole
drop in the camp oven and surround it with an even amount of embers including on top of the lid
cover the hole with earth and leave to bake for 1½ hours
dig up the oven and open it to reveal a golden crusted loaf of sweet-scented moist bread
devour with good friends

RICE CHAPATIS WITH TOASTED WALNUTS

I was taught to make these chapatis by Ken Israel, my friend and business partner of many years. He has made me many varieties over the years but the ones with walnuts, which I believe were the first ones I tried, are still my favorite. These are a great way to use leftover rice and a good reason for leaving some.

Take care when turning them over; they have a tendency to break. If you have one, use a solid cast-iron flat pan; if you do not have one, request one – they make a great gift. These are ideal for people wanting a wheat-free meal.

Serves 4 to 6
Season: all

2 cups well-cooked brown rice (note: 1 cup raw rice with 2 cups water and a pinch of salt will make 2 cups well-cooked rice)
3 tablespoons chopped toasted walnuts
1 large pinch salt
oil to just coat the pan

combine all ingredients except the oil
knead together with clean, damp hands
form a ball of the rice mixture
press into a flat circle the diameter of your frying pan
heat a heavy frying pan on a low heat and brush with only enough oil to coat the pan
put rice disc into pan and leave to cook 5 to 10 minutes
turn over carefully and repeat
cut like a pizza and eat as a snack or with miso cheese or soup

The end result will be crisp outer grains of rice and soft inner rice.

SOUPS

Spring miso soup

SPRING MISO SOUP

Vary this recipe by using whatever green spring vegetables you like. Try it with white miso for a lighter, sweeter taste. Always cook miso gently. The enzymes it contains, beneficial to good digestion, are assisted by gentle heat but are denatured by boiling. It is said that adding a pungent flavor such as ginger, lemon or green onion (scallion) stems to miso soup just before serving will activate the enzymes, making them more beneficial.

Serves 5 to 6
Season: spring

4 green onions (scallions)
½ bunch bok choy
3½ teaspoons corn oil
1-in (2.5-cm) fresh ginger, very finely sliced.
6-in (15-cm) stick kombu, soaked in water to cover for 30 minutes
6 cups (1.5 L) stock
3¼ oz (100 g) silken tofu, cut into small cubes
4 tablespoons brown rice (gen mai) miso

chop green onions into rounds, keeping the white and green parts separate
cut the bok choy, keeping the white and green parts separate
heat a pan and add the oil
sauté the white of onions, then the ginger
add the white of bok choy
drain and finely slice the kombu; combine the soaking water with stock
add the kombu and stock to the pan
simmer, uncovered, for 20 minutes
turn heat to low and add the silken tofu
mix the miso to a paste using a little of the soup
add the miso and the greens from the onions and bok choy
cook for 5 minutes; do not boil
serve with more ginger if desired

COOL AND CREAMY WATERCRESS SOUP

A cool soup in hot weather makes a light and refreshing meal.
Be sure to blend the greens well as this is best when it is very smooth.

Serves 6
Season: summer

2 tablespoons olive oil
2 leeks, white part only, finely sliced
3 cloves garlic, finely chopped
1/2 teaspoon grated nutmeg
5 oz (150 g) watercress, washed well and roughly chopped
5 oz (150 g) spinach, washed well and roughly chopped
1 teaspoon sea salt
8 cups (2 L) strong stock
3/4 cup plus 2 tablespoons (7 fl oz/120 ml) soy milk
1/4 teaspoon freshly ground black pepper, or to taste

heat a deep pan
add the olive oil
sauté the leeks until golden brown
add the garlic and cook 5 minutes
sprinkle in the nutmeg and stir
add the watercress, spinach and salt
turn the heat up a little
cook until watercress and spinach are bright green and collapsed
blend the watercress mixture until smooth
add the cold stock and soy milk and blend again
refrigerate until ready to serve
season with pepper and serve cold

SWEET CORN AND WAKAME SOUP

The sweetness of autumn-ripe sweet corn combines well with wakame and miso.
Vary the miso and see how different the soup will be.

Serves 4 to 5
Season: autumn

4½ teaspoons corn oil
1½ small leeks, finely sliced
1 cob sweet corn, kernels cut off
3½ teaspoons wakame flakes, soaked in water to cover
6 oz (175 g) tofu, cut into small cubes
2 tablespoons brown rice (gen mai) miso
4 cups (1 L) stock
1 tablespoon rice vinegar
1 teaspoon fish sauce (optional)
4 teaspoons finely chopped parsley or chives

heat a pan, add the oil
sauté the leeks until soft
stir in the corn kernels
drain the wakame; add soaking liquid to stock
add the wakame and tofu to the pan; cook 5 minutes, stirring
mix the miso with a little stock
add the stock, miso and vinegar
simmer for 20 minutes; do not boil
taste and add the fish sauce if you like
serve with parsley or chives

ROAST GARLIC AND ZUCCHINI SOUP

If you prefer, make this soup without garlic. Garlic has a dominant
flavor that is too strong for some people.

Serves 5 to 6
Season: autumn/winter

10 cloves garlic, unpeeled
3 large zucchini, sliced
3 tablespoons olive oil
½ teaspoon sea salt
2 onions, roughly chopped
½ leek, sliced
1 large potato, chopped
4 cups (1 L) stock
2 tablespoons toasted walnuts
2 teaspoons umeboshi vinegar

preheat oven to 400°F (200°C)
rub the garlic cloves and zucchini with 1 tablespoon olive oil
and a pinch of salt
place them on a baking sheet and roast for approximately 30 minutes, being
careful not to burn them
heat a large pan and pour in the remaining oil
sauté the onions and leek until both are soft and well cooked
stir in the potato and the rest of the salt
pour in the stock and simmer until the potatoes are soft
squeeze the garlic pulp out of the skins
discard the garlic skins
blend the garlic pulp and zucchini with the walnuts and umeboshi vinegar
add the potatoes and stock to the blender
continue to blend thoroughly
serve hot with crusty bread

SWIMMING NOODLES

Oden

Noodles are probably my favorite food. I am the "noodleaholic" among my friends. I keep many varieties of noodles in the cupboard and can be found looking to them for inspiration several nights a week, no matter what the season. I combine what I have in the fridge with the appropriate noodle to make a meal I am certain will be appreciated. As most noodles have an Asian origin I usually mix them with Asian ingredients and flavors.

There are many noodle varieties and each has its own unique flavor and texture.

Swimming noodles is my name for a combination of stock, vegetables and noodles.

There is a difference in the way pasta and noodles are eaten. With pasta the starch is desired as it assists the sauce to stick to the pasta and the shape of the pasta is designed to suit the type of sauce it will be eaten with.

Asian noodles are washed thoroughly under cold running water after cooking to remove the starch and then they are reheated in boiling stock before serving or adding to soup. This produces a slippery texture that is easily digested. I wash noodles that are to be eaten with a dipping sauce, as otherwise they become quite sticky. I don't wash noodles when I cook them together with other ingredients in a stock. If the noodles are fresh and of high quality, the starch adds flavor and slightly thickens the stock.

Allow approximately 2½ oz (80 g) per person if serving noodles alone and 1½ to 2 oz (50 to 60 g) per person in a dish that contains a stock and other bulky ingredients.

ODEN (TRADITIONAL JAPANESE WINTER STREET FOOD)

On the streets of Tokyo in deepest winter, Oden vendors stand in thick snow beside old-fashioned carts. The ingredients are arranged in a shallow cast-iron tray, kept warm by coals below. Different ingredients are displayed in a stock and cold passers-by may stop and choose the items they favor for a quick snack or a meal. Japanese culture dictates that food is eaten on the spot rather than as you move about, so the chosen items are put together in a china bowl with some of the simmering stock. A warm glass of sake may also be offered. Standing beside the firebox at 2 am, holding the warm bowl and sipping the stock is one of my fondest memories of the time I spent in Japan.

Serves 6
Season: winter

FOR THE POCKETS AND CABBAGE ROLLS
2 tablespoons sesame oil
1 large onion, cut in half and thinly sliced
½ large carrot, grated
½ daikon, grated
½ burdock root (gobo), grated
½ large lotus root, grated
½ teaspoon sea salt
6½ oz (200 g) wet bean thread noodles (shirataki)
1 packet of 3 deep-fried tofu skins (abura age) cut in half
6 large green leaves (cabbage or Chinese greens)
kampyo (dried gourd strips) for tying parcels

FOR THE BROTH
3 (12-in/30-cm) sticks kombu, wiped and soaked 20 minutes, reserve soaking liquid
6 whole fresh or dried shiitake mushrooms, with stems removed (soak for 20 minutes if using dried mushrooms and reserve soaking liquid)
2 large carrots, cut into thick rounds
1 daikon, cut into thick rounds
1 large lotus root, cut into medium-thick rounds
1 cup (8 fl oz/250 ml) tamari
1 cup (8 fl oz/250 ml) mirin
zest of 1 large lemon, cut into strips
1 teaspoon sea salt
½ bunch green onions (scallions) or garlic chives
6½ oz (200 g) somen or udon noodles, cooked, drained and rinsed

optional ingredients:
6 eggs
6 small chicken thighs
6 pieces firm white-fleshed fish or fishballs
6 pieces tofu, fried
6 slices yam paste (konyaku), cut into lengths

heat a frying pan; add oil
sauté the onion slices until smell changes
add grated vegetables; cook 5 minutes stirring
combine with salt and drained shirataki noodles and set aside
pour boiling water over the tofu skins to remove excess oil
drain, then cut in half and open each half to make six pockets
blanch the cabbage leaves in boiling salted water
drain and refresh under cold running water
stuff each pocket and each cabbage leaf with one-twelfth of the fried mixture
fold over top and tie each pocket with a gourd strip
set stuffed pockets aside, covered
cut kombu into $4\frac{3}{4}$ in x 2 in (12 cm x 5 cm) lengths
roll this kombu into 12 tubes and tie each with a strip of gourd
lay the remaining kombu strips on the bottom of a large, deep frying pan
place the shiitake mushrooms and other vegetables in the pan
cover with the soaking water from the shiitake and kombu and extra water if needed
pour in the tamari and mirin
add the lemon zest and the kombu rolls
bring to a simmer, covered, and cook very gently for 2 hours
add the tofu pockets and the cabbage rolls
continue to cook for another hour
toward the end of the cooking time add the other ingredients you have chosen
top up with water to keep all ingredients covered as they cook
serve in deep bowls
let each person choose their items and pour a little of the stock over their food
place chopped green onions or garlic chives in a bowl for people to add

Serve some light sour vegetable pickles or a simple boiled salad as a side dish to offset the deep flavors in this dish. You can produce a good broth in 1 hour but an intense flavor is derived from long, slow simmering. This looks far more complex than it is to make. If you want to simplify the dish eliminate the pockets and cabbage rolls, and leave the kombu in strips.

COLD SOMEN NOODLES WITH LEMON DIPPING SAUCE

This dish is a variation on Japanese summer noodle dishes. It has a cooling effect on the system, and if you enjoy strong spicy flavors, add some wasabi to the dipping sauce. Serve small mounds on the side of each plate and let people add as much or as little as they choose. Soba noodles are extremely good eaten this way too.

Serves 4
Season: summer

1½ cups (12 fl oz/400 ml) water
½ cup plus 2 tablespoons (5 fl oz/150 ml) tamari
3 tablespoons (1½ fl oz/50 ml) lemon juice
8 oz (250 g) somen noodles, cooked and rinsed in cold water
2 sheets toasted nori, cut into small strips, using scissors
1 bunch chives, finely chopped

combine the water, tamari and lemon juice
refrigerate until ready to serve
arrange the somen noodles in the center of 4 flat serving plates
pour the dipping sauce into four small soup bowls
top the noodles with the nori and chives
pick up a few noodles at a time with chopsticks, put them into the dipping sauce then take the bowl to your mouth and eat

BROTHS

Oyster mushroom rice noodle broth with prawns

A broth for me is a means to consume the essence of the ingredients it contains. By cooking ingredients together the flavors mingle and if well combined they have a synergistic effect, with each item detectable, none overriding the overall taste, each supporting the other.

In summer the broth is quickly made from light ingredients, in winter long, slow cooking and cooking under pressure produces a richer result with soft grains and collapsed root vegetables that offer warmth and satisfaction.

Serves 6
Season: summer

6 cups (1.5 L) vegetable or fish stock
2 cups (16 fl oz/500 ml) prawn stock
¾-in (2-cm) fresh ginger, finely sliced
¾-in (2-cm) piece galangal, finely sliced
1½ oz (50 g) flat green beans, finely
sliced diagonally
1 lb (500 g) fresh rice noodles, cut
into 1-in (2.5-cm) strips
5 oz (150 g) oyster mushrooms,
finely sliced
6 large or 18 small green prawns
peeled, tails on
3 tablespoons lime juice
4½ teaspoons shoyu (optional)
4½ teaspoons fish sauce (optional)
1 bunch fresh cilantro (coriander),
leaves only
3 teaspoons prawn oil (see below)
1 large lime, cut into 6 pieces

combine the stocks in a large pan with
the ginger and galangal
bring to a simmer
skim any scum that rises to the surface
discard the ginger and galangal
add the beans and cook for 1 minute
add the rice noodles and bring back to
a simmer
add the mushrooms and prawns, cook
for 3 minutes
taste and season with the lime juice and
a little shoyu or fish sauce if needed
drop in the cilantro leaves as you serve
drizzle ½ teaspoon prawn oil on top of
the broth in each bowl
give each person a piece of lime to
squeeze into the broth

PRAWN OIL

3 tablespoons olive oil
1 large white onion, finely sliced
½ leek, white part only, finely sliced
1 large carrot, finely chopped
2 celery sticks, finely chopped
2 large tomatoes, finely chopped
heads and shells of 18 prawns
¾ cup plus 2 tablespoons white wine
¾ cup plus 2 tablespoons olive oil
2 cups (16 fl oz/500 ml) water

heat a heavy pan
add 3 tablespoons olive oil
sauté all the vegetables in the oil
add the prawn heads and shells

mash with a heavy wooden spoon
cook until beginning to caramelize
pour in white wine and reduce until it
becomes syrupy
add the remaining olive oil and the water
simmer and reduce until only the oil
remains
strain through a fine sieve or cheesecloth
let stand 10 minutes
scoop the oil from the top and discard
the rest
this is the prawn oil
use as a garnish with fish soup and broths
keep in a sealed glass jar in the
refrigerator or freeze in small batches

COCONUT-SPICED TOFU BROTH

You can make this as mild or spicy as you like. I prefer it only so strong that
I can still taste all the ingredients; I dislike food that contains so much chile,
the effect is burning heat alone. You could add shellfish, fish or chicken to
this broth for variety.

Serves 6
Season: summer

11 oz (350 g) firm tofu
peanut oil for deep-frying
5 tablespoons (2½ fl oz/70 ml) peanut oil
2 onions, diced
3 large cloves garlic, finely chopped
1½ inches (3 cm) fresh ginger, finely chopped
1 bunch cilantro (coriander), leaves and stems finely chopped and kept separate
2 teaspoons green curry paste
1 lb (500 g) sweet potatoes, diced large
2½ cups (20 fl oz/600 ml) coconut milk
1 tablespoon fish sauce or brown rice miso
3 cups (24 fl oz/750 ml) Asian vegetable stock (page 46)
6½ oz (200 g) rice vermicelli
3 kaffir lime leaves
2 lemons, cut into wedges

cut the tofu into bite-sized triangles
deep-fry the tofu in peanut oil until it has a golden skin
drain well and set aside
heat a deep pan and add the 5 tablespoons peanut oil
sauté the onions until soft and golden brown
stir in the garlic, ginger and cilantro stems, cook 5 minutes
add the green curry paste and sweet potatoes; sauté a further 5 minutes
pour in the coconut milk and fish sauce or miso
add the stock and fried tofu
simmer for 30 minutes
cook the rice vermicelli in boiling water, drain and rinse well with hot water
put the vermicelli in a warmed bowl
add half the chopped cilantro leaves and all the lime leaves to the broth
serve broth in deep bowls
serve vermicelli, lemon wedges and the remaining cilantro leaves in separate bowls
for people to help themselves

CHINESE VEGETABLE BROTH

This is a simplified version of a wonderful Chinese-Malaysian dish taught to me by Oi-fa, one of the first employees at Iku. She is a superb cook who taught me a great deal about Asian ingredients. We ate Yum Cha together and we shopped in Chinatown for ingredients I had difficulty believing were edible. Eat this over rice or noodles or as a soup.

Serves 5 to 6
Season: autumn/winter

5 shiitake mushrooms (with stems removed), soaked in
2 cups (16 fl oz/500 ml) boiling water for 1 hour
⅓ oz (10 g) dried black fungus, soaked in cold water for 1 hour
1½ oz (50 g) lily buds, soaked in cold water for 1 hour
2½ oz (80 g) dried tofu sticks, soaked in boiling water for 1 hour
3 tablespoons salted black beans, soaked in boiling water for 10 minutes
8 cups (2 L) water, including shiitake soaking liquid
1½ oz (50 g) Chinese red dates
¼ cup plus 3 tablespoons (3½ fl oz/100 ml) Chinese rice wine (chiew)
¼ cup plus 3 tablespoons (3½ fl oz/100 ml) mirin
1 tablespoon grated palm sugar
¾ cup (6 fl oz/180 ml) tamari
1 teaspoon sea salt
1½ oz (50 g) bean thread noodles, broken up
1 bunch chives, cut into 4-in (10-cm) lengths

drain mushrooms and add soaking liquid to water, finely slice mushrooms
drain tofu sticks and set aside
drain black fungus and finely slice
drain lily buds; remove and discard the hard end and tie each bud in a knot
bring a pan of water to a simmer
boil the tofu sticks for 15 minutes or until they are soft and creamy white
drain tofu and chop into 1-in (2.5-cm) pieces, discarding any hard pieces
drain black beans and rinse well
bring the water including mushroom liquid to a simmer in a large pan
add all the ingredients except the bean thread noodles and chives
bring back to a simmer and cook gently for a minimum of 1 hour
add the noodles and cook another 5 minutes or so
serve garnished with chives

PRESSURE-COOKED BARLEY BROTH
WITH ROOT VEGETABLES

This is a homey meal and reminds me of the lamb stews my mother made and served with red cabbage pickle. The sharpness of the vinegar in the pickle offset and complemented the fat in the stew. I seldom cook with meat and prefer this vegan version with no fat, but I still enjoy the pickle as a condiment.

Serves 6
Season: winter

2 tablespoons sesame oil
1 large onion, diced
2 leeks, sliced
3 large cloves garlic, finely chopped
1½ inches (3 cm) fresh ginger, finely chopped
1½ large potatoes, cut into large chunks
2½ large carrots, roll cut
1 cup diced parsnips
1 cup (6½ oz/200 g) pearl barley, soaked for 4 hours and drained well
2½ cups (20 fl oz/600 ml) stock of your choice (fish stock is very good in this dish)
1½ teaspoons tamari
1½ teaspoons umeboshi vinegar

heat a pressure cooker and add the oil
sauté the onions until soft and translucent
add the leeks and cook until soft
add the garlic and ginger; stir well and cook for 5 minutes
stir in the root vegetables and coat with oil
pour in the barley
add the stock, tamari and umeboshi vinegar
bring to full-pressure, turn down and cook for 30 minutes
allow the pressure to drop
stir gently to combine the ingredients
serve with lots of dark green vegetables

Witlof and orange with curly kale

BLANCHED FAVA BEAN AND GOLDEN ZUCCHINI SALAD

If you are feeling loving and you have the time, cook the fava beans and then peel off the skins. It is not necessary to do this, but peeled fava beans have a softer texture and a sweeter flavor. This salad makes a good light lunch if you add some pasta or cooked grain to it.

Serves 6
Season: spring

2 large golden zucchini, cut in half lengthways and sliced into half moons
1 lb (500 g) shelled fava (broad) beans
4 tablespoons olive oil
2 large yellow (brown) onions, sliced lengthways into fine crescents
¼ teaspoon coarse sea salt
3 drops pure lemon oil

heat a pan of water
blanch the zucchini first, then the beans
refresh in cold water, drain and set aside
heat a heavy frying pan
add the olive oil
sauté the onions until caramelized
add zucchini, beans, salt and lemon oil
serve warm or cold

ROMANO BEANS WITH NEW POTATO SALAD

Serves 6
Season: summer

¾ lb (12 oz/400 g) new potatoes, pontiac when possible
¾ cup romano beans (wide, flat and long green beans) sliced on diagonal ½-in (1-cm) wide
6 basil leaves
pinch sea salt
grind of fresh black pepper
2 tablespoons extra-virgin olive oil

boil the potatoes in lots of salted water
drain and cool
slice potatoes in half unless they are very small; set aside
blanch the beans
refresh in cold water and set aside
tear the basil leaves into small pieces; set aside
arrange the vegetables on a large plate
sprinkle with sea salt
grind pepper over the top
drizzle with olive oil
throw on the basil leaves and serve

WITLOF AND ORANGE WITH CURLY KALE

This is my exception to the "no fruit in salads" rule. I think it may be that this was a salad my mother made, but it might just be that these flavors suit each other so well. The slightly bitter taste of the witlof and curly kale is soothed by the sweetness of the citrus fruit.

Serves 6
Season: autumn/winter

½ head (6½ oz/200 g) curly kale, washed and well drained

1 red and 2 white heads (11 oz/350 g) witlof (Belgian endive), washed and well drained

segments of 1 orange, removed from their membranes

zest of 1 orange, grated

pinch sea salt

cut the curly kale into edible pieces without bruising
blanch quickly in salted water
refresh in cold water
cut the witlof into long thin slices
mix the orange segments with the leaves
combine the zest and salt with the leaves and orange segments
set aside and serve with green herb dressing (page 162)

WARM BAKED ROOT VEGETABLES AND KOMBU SALAD

Some may say this is not really a salad, as they define salads as raw ingredients of the lettuce family. I believe when it is very cold and the nights are long, that this warming vegetable dish is an adequate replacement for raw food that cools the body more than desired at this time of year.

Serves 6
Season: winter

6-in (15-cm) stick kombu, soaked in ¾ cup plus 2 tablespoons cold water

¾ cup plus 2 tablespoons vegetable stock or the kombu soaking water

3½ teaspoons tamari

1 lb (500 g) pumpkin, cut into wedges

2 large carrots, roll cut

6½ oz (200 g) celeriac, cut into large dice

2 cups roll cut parsnips

preheat oven to 400°F (200°C)
place the kombu in a baking dish with the stock and tamari
lay the vegetables on the top
place, uncovered, in oven
bake for 30 to 40 minutes
serve each person with vegetables and a little kombu

Italian portobello polenta

ONE-POT MEALS

As the title suggests these meals are made in a single pan. This saves cleanup time and is also useful for camping trips.

They are simple meals that can be prepared quickly, and once the preparation is done, you can leave them to cook while you do something else. This style of cooking is great when you have a few people to feed but you also have other things to do.

You can eat these dishes as they are, or embellish them with the addition of salads or vegetables. Vary the stocks used in the recipes to see which you prefer. Grains suit one-pot cooking as they combine so well with many other ingredients.

ITALIAN PORTOBELLO POLENTA

Keep the heat low and the pot covered; give it a stir with a long-handled wooden spoon now and then as you pass by.

Serves 6
Season: autumn

POLENTA
3 tablespoons olive oil
1 large onion, diced
6 cloves garlic, finely chopped
1⅓ cups polenta
7 cups (1.8 L) stock
1 cup (2½ oz/80 g) Parmesan cheese, grated or ½ teaspoon sea salt

MUSHROOM TOPPING
½ cup (4 fl oz/125 ml) olive oil
3 portobello mushrooms, sliced
20 small button mushrooms
18 Swiss brown mushrooms, cut in half or in quarters if very large
6 cloves garlic, finely chopped
5 tablespoons (2½ fl oz/80 ml) soy milk
¼ teaspoon black pepper
½ teaspoon sea salt

to make polenta, heat a large pan
add oil and sauté onion until quite soft
stir in the garlic and mix well
cook 5 minutes
pour in the polenta and coat with oil
stir for a minute until well mixed
ladle in the stock
add the sea salt if not using the Parmesan cheese
whisk the polenta mixture
bring to a simmer
stir often, for 40 minutes or until it is the consistency of pourable porridge
if using Parmesan, add it at this stage
to make mushroom topping, heat a large frying pan
add oil
sauté all mushrooms together, then add garlic
stir in the soy milk, season with pepper and salt and cook until tender
spoon polenta into shallow bowls and top with mushrooms

STEAMED SUMMER VEGETABLES WITH LEMON TAHINI SAUCE

This is a summer version of a simple dish. You may use whatever vegetables are available in any season and try another sauce. Black bean sauce with deep-fried walnuts over cabbage and root vegetables was a version I served in autumn and winter in my first restaurant, Manna, where it was very well received.

Serves 6
Season: summer

SUMMER VEGETABLES
$^3/_4$ lb (12 oz/400 g) new potatoes, boiled and peeled
2 cobs sweet corn sliced into 1$^1/_4$-in (3-cm) rounds
$^1/_2$ lb green beans, each sliced into 3 pieces
$^1/_2$ Chinese cabbage, sliced into 2.5-cm (1-in) pieces
2 heads broccoli, cut into florets
3 large zucchini, sliced on the diagonal into 1-in (2.5-cm) pieces

LEMON TAHINI SAUCE
$^1/_2$ cup plus 2 tablespoons (5 fl oz/150 ml) hulled tahini
$^1/_4$ cup (2 fl oz/60 ml) lemon juice
2 teaspoons umeboshi vinegar
1 tablespoon shoyu
$^3/_4$ cup plus 2 tablespoon (7 fl oz/200 ml) boiling vegetable stock

bring a large steamer to a rolling boil
steam the vegetables in the order given, by adding each one a little before the last one has cooked
meanwhile, make the tahini sauce
combine all the ingredients and whisk well to a smooth sauce
drain the vegetables and serve with the sauce

RED RICE UNDER PRESSURE WITH

SHIITAKE MUSHROOM SAUCE

It is quite possible to make this without a pressure cooker. Turn the heat as low as it will go, and add 30 minutes to the cooking time. This dish is quite red, and contrasts well with cauliflower and greens.

Serves 4 to 5
Season: autumn/winter

½ cup (3½ oz/100 g) adzuki beans, washed and soaked in cold water 2 hours
4-in (10-cm) stick kombu
3 shiitake mushrooms, with stems removed, broken into pieces
1½ cups (9½ oz/300 g) brown rice, washed and drained
½ teaspoon sea salt
4½ cups (1.12 L) water

SHIITAKE MUSHROOM SAUCE
3 cups (24 fl oz/750 ml) soy milk
3 shiitake mushrooms, with stems removed, soaked in 1 cup (8 fl oz/250 ml)
boiling water, drained and finely sliced
1 cup (8 fl oz/250 ml) shiitake mushroom soaking liquid
pinch sea salt
4½ teapoons tamari
1 tablespoon ginger juice
2 tablespoons kudzu or cornstarch (cornflour), dissolved in 4 tablespoons cold water

place beans, kombu, shiitake pieces and rice into pressure cooker
add sea salt and water
bring to full-pressure
turn to low
cook 1 hour
remove lid and stir gently to combine ingredients
re-cover and allow to stand for 5 minutes
serve with steamed or baked vegetables and shiitake mushroom sauce
to make the mushroom sauce, warm the soy milk and mushroom water together
add the shiitake mushroom slices with the salt and tamari
bring to a simmer and cook for 5 minutes
add the ginger juice
whisk in the kudzu or cornstarch slurry
cook until the sauce is smooth and thickened

BAKED MILLET AND GINGER DAIKON

This is an incredibly easy dish to make – it is quickly put together and can be left alone to cook. If you want to embellish it, make a shiitake mushroom sauce (page 94) to go with it.

Serves 6
Season: autumn/winter

2 tablespoons sesame oil
1 onion, diced
1½ cups (10 oz/320 g) hulled millet
2 tablespoons grated fresh ginger
3 cups diced pumpkin
1⅓ oz (40 g) arame
1 (5-in/13-cm length) daikon, cut in half lengthways and sliced into half moons
4 cups (1 L) vegetable stock
½ teaspoon sea salt
1½ teaspoons tamari
1½ teaspoons umeboshi vinegar

heat a heavy ovenproof pan with a well-fitting lid
preheat the oven to 350°F (180°C)
add the oil to the pan
sauté the onions until soft and translucent
add the millet and ginger, coat with oil and stir gently
continue to stir and cook until the millet is golden and smells nutty
add the pumpkin, arame and daikon
in a separate pan bring the stock, salt, tamari and umeboshi vinegar to a boil
pour the boiling stock into the millet mixture, being careful of the steam
stir well and cover the pan
place in the oven for approximately 1 hour
carefully remove from the oven, take off the lid and stir gently to combine all the ingredients
serve hot with steamed greens

CASSEROLES

Fennel, potato and mustard casserole

I use the term casserole to define a dish that is a combination of legumes (that is beans, peas or lentils) and vegetables, cooked together and eaten with grain. The legume/grain combination provides a delicious balanced meal. Legumes have a high protein, fat and carbohydrate content, and are also rich in calcium, several B vitamins and potassium. Sprouted legumes can provide vitamin C and enzymes.

It is worth checking the fundamentals section of the book to read about beans and how best to cook them (page 57). Many people fear eating legumes, assuming they will be poorly digested. But the main causes of poorly digested beans are improper cooking techniques, insufficient chewing and poor combinations of ingredients. Well-cooked beans make wonderful dishes that will have people asking for more.

FAVA BEAN, LEMON AND GARLIC CASSEROLE

Although these beans are fresh, I include them here because of their substantial nature. When they are available fresh in spring I like to use them as often as possible because the season for organically produced fava beans seems too short to me. Use them boiled in salads or boil them and have a feast on them with a little olive oil, lemon juice and sea salt.

Serves 6
Season: spring

2 tablespoons olive oil
4 onions, cut into wedges
3 cloves garlic, roughly chopped
1 cup (8 fl oz/250 ml) strong vegetable, fish or chicken stock
2 tablespoons lemon juice
½ teaspoon sea salt
½ cup (3½ oz/100 g) borlotti beans, shelled and boiled until soft
2½ cups (10 oz/320 g) fava (broad) beans, shelled and boiled until soft
2 cups (9½ oz/300 g) sliced green beans, cut on the diagonal and blanched

heat a pan
add oil
sauté the onions until soft
add garlic; cook 5 minutes
pour in the stock, lemon juice and salt
boil uncovered, until no liquid remains and the onion is frying again in oil
stir in all the beans
cook for 5 minutes
serve with rice, quinoa or other grain

GARBANZO, SWEET CORN AND CILANTRO CASSEROLE

The basis for this dish was taught to me by Eli, a beautiful Israeli woman who
worked with us at Iku for several years. To me, it is a magic combination of
flavors and textures, what I call a marriage of ingredients – those made
for one another.

Serves 6
Season: summer

1¼ cups garbanzos (chickpeas), soaked in cold water 4 to 12 hours
2 tablespoons olive oil
3 yellow (brown) onions, cut into wedges
1 leek, green part only, cut into thick slices, washed and drained
2 orange sweet potatoes, unpeeled, cut into chunks
1 large cob sweet corn, kernels cut off
3 large cloves garlic, finely chopped and kept separate
1½ bunches cilantro (coriander), leaves roughly chopped, stems finely chopped
and kept separate from each other
6 cups (1.5 L) stock
2 tablespoons umeboshi vinegar
½ teaspoon sea salt

cook the garbanzos carefully until they are quite soft (this should
take approximately 1 hour), drain well and set aside
heat a large, deep frying pan
pour in the oil
add the onion wedges and fry for 5 minutes
add the leek to the pan and continue to cook
add the sweet potatoes and the corn kernels
turn the heat to low
add the garlic and cilantro stems and sauté with the vegetables
add the stock, umeboshi vinegar, and salt
simmer, uncovered, until the liquid has reduced by half
remove one-third of the mixture
blend and return to the pan
fold in the cilantro leaves
reheat and serve with sourdough bread, steamed rice or millet

FENNEL, POTATO AND MUSTARD CASSEROLE

The important thing with this dish is to roast the vegetables until they are very soft and browned. Cooked in this way, they will contribute to the moisture and intensity of flavor in the dish. I have made the dish with Jerusalem artichokes and potatoes instead of beans and that was very good too.

Serves 6
Season: winter

1 large fennel bulb
3/4 lb (12 oz/400 g) pinkeye or other waxy potato, washed well with skins left on
4 cloves garlic, chopped
2 tablespoons olive oil
1/2 teaspoon sea salt
2 tablespoons Dijon mustard
1/4 cup plus 3 tablespoons (3 1/2 fl oz/100 ml) stock
1 tablespoon lemon juice
1/4 teaspoon black pepper
1 cup navy (haricot) beans, soaked and cooked until tender
1/2 bunch fresh fennel leaves

cut the fennel and potatoes in half and then into wedges
place in a baking dish
add the garlic
rub the oil and salt into the cut vegetables
add the mustard, stock, lemon juice and pepper and mix through to coat evenly
bake at 335°F (170°C) for about 35 minutes or until the vegetables are golden brown and collapsing; turn twice during cooking
add the navy beans and continue to cook for a further 15 minutes
serve with sprigs of fresh fennel leaves

WHOLE OAT, PUMPKIN AND ADZUKI BEAN CASSEROLE

Pumpkin and adzuki beans are another great combination; the sweet flavors combine well and are offset by the warmth of the ginger. Whole oats, when well cooked, have a soft chewy texture that suits the softness of the other ingredients. Oats are said to be beneficial for the skin and the combination of adzuki beans and pumpkin is good for the kidneys.

Whole oats are also good in bread; cook them well before adding them to your dough.

Serves 6
Season: winter

6½ oz (200 g) adzuki beans, soaked overnight in cold water
1¼ cups whole oats/groats, soaked overnight in cold water
2½-in (6-cm) stick kombu, cut into fine strips
1 tablespoon sesame oil
½ large onion, cut into wedges
2½ inches (3 cm) fresh ginger, finely chopped
3 cups medium diced pumpkin
1 tablespoon tamari
2 cups (16 fl oz/500 ml) vegetable stock
½ bunch parsley, leaves only

combine the adzuki beans, oats and kombu in a pan
cover with fresh cold water
cook until quite soft
drain, set aside and keep the cooking liquid
heat a pan and add the oil
sauté the onions until soft and brown
add the ginger and pumpkin and cook for 5 minutes
pour in the tamari, stock and cooking liquid
bring to a simmer and cook until the pumpkin is tender
add the beans, oats and kombu mixture and bring to a simmer, being careful not to burn the beans
serve hot
add the parsley to the top of each serving

PASTRY, PIES, TARTS AND PASTIES

Natto miso and ginger pumpkin tartlet

Pasties have a wonderful history: they were conceived and made by the wives of tin miners in Cornwall when barley was the staple grain. Pastry made from barley flour is more durable than wheat — it needed to be, as these pastry packages were dropped down the mine shaft in time for lunch. The thick rolled edge acted as a handle, so the miners' filthy fingers did not contaminate their meal. Sometimes a pasty housed a savory filling at one end and a sweet filling at the other where initials had been crafted from pastry and stuck down so the owner could identify his pasty and also ascertain the location of the portion to eat first.

Today barley pastry is unheard of — it's too dry and heavy for the modern palate — but the pasty has endured and today is made with rich, delectable fillings rather than meager potatoes, an onion and possibly a few scraps of lamb.

Pastry has many forms; here I offer a very small sampling. Experiment with the ratios of fat to flour and liquid, and you will begin to see the possibilities. The type of fat you choose will make a huge difference to the end result. It's easier to make pastry with oil than with butter, because you can be less concerned about the temperature of hands, counter and ingredients. Butterless pastry can have great texture and flavor. But it does taste different; I prefer it when I want a less clinging pastry that I can be sure is kinder on my arteries.

Subtle changes can be made by using different oils. I like cold-pressed corn oil for sweet shortcrust pastry; it has a wonderful dark yellow color. Virgin olive oil has a buttery flavor that I enjoy in savory pastry, and in cakes. Pastry can be made in advance, portioned and frozen to use as you need it.

Shortcrust is a crumbly pastry, fairly rich with oil.

Hot water pastry is light, hard and crisp. It is easy to work with. Leavened pastry is pliable to work; it is light to eat and has a good flavor.

SHORT SHORTCRUST PASTRY

Makes 1 lb 3 oz (600 g)
Season: autumn/winter

2½ cups (11 oz/350 g) unbleached
white flour
2 tablespoons (1 oz/30 g) rice flour
½ teaspoon sea salt
4 tablespoons (2½ fl oz/80 ml) olive oil
¾ cup plus 3 tablespoons cold water
Soy milk or egg wash to glaze

combine all the dry ingredients
thoroughly
pour the olive oil into the flours
roughly rub in the oil so some clumps
of oil and flour remain
sprinkle in the water, a little at a time
press the mix together
knead briefly
rest, covered by a clean cloth for 1 hour
roll out on a well-floured board
bake at 400°F (200°C) for
approximately 20 minutes
brush with soy milk or egg wash
bake for a further 10 to 15 minutes
until golden brown

LEAVENED PASTRY

Makes 2 lb (1 kg)
Season: all

2 cups (8 oz/250 g) whole-wheat pastry
flour
2¼ cups (9½ oz/300 g) unbleached
white flour
½ cup (4 fl oz/125 ml) olive oil
1 cup (8 fl oz/250 ml) leaven (page 63)
1 cup (8 fl oz/250 ml) filtered water
pinch sea salt, dissolved in the water

sift the flours together
rub the oil evenly into the flours
pour in the leaven and mix by hand
add the water and bring the mix
together
knead to a smooth ball
allow to rest, covered, for 1 hour
roll to desired shape
allow to rise, covered, in a warm spot
for 30 minutes
bake in a hot oven 400°F (200°C) for
approximately 30 minutes until golden
brown

CRISP HOT WATER PASTRY

This pastry is ideal for individual crisp tartlets. It is brittle and does not easily absorb liquid. You will need 2 oz (60 g) pastry per 4½-in (11-cm) tart pan.

Makes 1 lb 3 oz (600 g)
Season: spring/summer

2 cups plus 3 tablespoons unbleached white flour
3½ oz (100 g) toasted sesame seeds (hulled)
¼ cup plus 3 tablespoons (3½ fl oz/100 ml) sesame oil
½ cup plus 2 tablespoons (5 fl oz/150 ml) boiling water
2 tablespoons tamari

combine all the dry ingredients
blend the wet ingredients to a creamy emulsion
mix the wet slowly with the dry
knead for a couple of minutes to combine
rest under a dry cloth for 30 minutes
roll out pastry to fit tart pan
bake at 400°F (200°C) for approximately 15 minutes until an even golden brown

ROAST VEGETABLE AND PECAN PIE

Serves 6
Season: autumn/winter

1½ lb (750 g) kabocha pumpkin, cut into irregular wedges
¾ lb (12 oz/400 g) sweet potato, cut into irregular wedges
2 leeks, cut in half lengthways and sliced into half moons
1½ cups diced eggplant
1 teaspoon sea salt
3 tablespoons olive oil
5 drops lemon oil
3½ oz (100 g) pecans, lightly toasted
8 oz (250 g) shortcrust or leavened pastry (page 106)
soy milk or egg wash to glaze

preheat the oven to 400°F (200°C)
combine all the vegetables in a large baking dish
rub in the salt and both oils
place in the oven and bake for 30 minutes or until vegetables are soft and beginning to brown
allow to cool in the dish
mix the pecans through the vegetables
roll out the pastry into two rounds
line an 8-in (20-cm) pie dish with one pastry round
fill with the vegetable mixture
cover with the other pastry round
pinch the edges together
trim the excess pastry
cut a cross in the center
brush with soy milk or egg wash to glaze
bake for 20 to 30 minutes
cool a little before removing from the dish
serve hot or cold

NATTO MISO AND GINGER PUMPKIN TARTLETS

Serves 6
Season: autumn/winter

2 cups (16 fl oz/500 ml) stock
3 tablespoons olive oil
4 onions, sliced into wedges
⁴/₅-inch (2-cm) fresh ginger, finely sliced
¼ pickled lemon
1 lb (500 g) kabocha pumpkin, peeled and cut into small wedges
½ teaspoon sea salt
4½ teaspoons barley (natto) miso
¼ lb green beans, finely sliced diagonally
9 oz (280 g) crisp hot water pastry (page 107), baked in a 12-in (30-cm) tart pan,
or 11 oz (360 g) pastry, baked in 6 (2-in/5-cm) tartlet pans

combine the stock with 2 tablespoons of oil, the onions, ginger and lemon pickle
bring to a simmer, uncovered
cook slowly until no liquid is left and the onions are very soft and frying in the oil
fry them a further 10 minutes
meanwhile, rub the pumpkin with the salt and the remaining tablespoon of oil
bake approximately 35 minutes in a 400°F (200°C) oven until the pumpkin is soft
and starting to brown
remove from the oven
mix the natto miso through the pumpkin carefully and set aside
blanch the green beans
refresh in cold water, drain well and set aside
combine the pumpkin and onion mixtures
fill the prebaked tart pan with the pumpkin mixture, top with
green beans and serve

ASPARAGUS AND TOFU-CHEESE TART

Serves 6
Season: spring/summer

2 tablespoons olive oil
2 leeks, washed and drained well, finely sliced
3 cloves garlic, finely chopped
1 large cob sweet corn, kernels cut off
6½ oz (200 g) tofu cheese, crumbled (see miso soy cheese on page 140)
9 oz (280 g) asparagus, cut into diagonal slices
½ oz (15 g) arame, soaked in boiling water 10 minutes and drained well
2 teaspoons shoyu
1 tablespoon balsamic vinegar
6½ oz (200 g) shortcrust or leavened pastry (page 106), baked
in a 12-in (30-cm) tart pan

heat a frying pan
add the oil
sauté the leek until quite soft but not brown
add the garlic and the corn kernels
cook for 5 minutes
crumble the tofu cheese into the pan
cook gently for a further 5 minutes; set aside to cool
blanch the asparagus
plunge into cold water and drain well; set aside
heat a small pan
add the arame
stir gently
pour in the shoyu and balsamic vinegar
cook 2 minutes and set aside
spread the tart shell with the tofu-cheese mixture
place the asparagus in the center
put the arame around the outer edge
serve soon after filling

SWEET POTATO AND POPPYSEED PASTIES

Makes 8 pasties
Season: autumn

3 tablespoons peanut oil
1 large onion, cut into wedges
4 cloves garlic, roughly chopped
½ teaspoon ground cumin
1½ lb (700 g) sweet potatoes, peeled and cut into large dice
1½ cups (12 fl oz/400 ml) coconut milk
1½ cups (12 fl oz/400 ml) stock
1 teaspoon sea salt or 1 tablespoon fish sauce
2 tablespoons lime juice
2 lb (1 kg) of shortcrust or leavened pastry (page 106) with 2 tablespoons
poppyseeds included
soy milk or egg wash to glaze

preheat oven to 350°F (180°C)
heat a large, deep frying pan
add the oil
fry the onions until softened and beginning to brown
add the garlic and cook for a few minutes
add the cumin and the sweet potatoes
stir well for 2 minutes
add the coconut milk, stock, salt or fish sauce and the lime juice
simmer over medium heat until the liquid has reduced to a thick sauce and the
sweet potato is breaking apart
cool before making into pasties
cut the dough into 8 pieces
roll out each piece on a floured board
use a bread and butter plate to cut each piece into a circle
place an eighth of the filling in the center of each round
pull the edges together and pinch and push to form the pasty's edge
place on an oiled baking sheet
bake for 15 minutes
brush with soy milk or egg wash to glaze
continue to bake a further 5 minutes
remove from the oven and serve hot or cold

EGGS

Steamed ginkgo nut custards with salmon

STEAMED GINKGO NUT CUSTARDS WITH SALMON

These unusual savory custards are a real treat and make a good impression without a lot of fuss. Try using mushrooms, scallops or chicken in place of the salmon, or leave out the ginkgo nuts if you find them too strongly flavored or hard to find. Use vegetable stock if you prefer. The belly of salmon is delicious in these custards but you could use any other cut instead.

Makes 6 custards
Season: all

2 organic free-range eggs
1 cup (8 fl oz/260 ml) dashi #1 or dashi #2 (page 45), cooled
½ cup (4 fl oz/120 ml) mirin
4½ teaspoons shoyu
6 ginkgo nuts, boiled, drained and sliced into 6 pieces
6 small shiitake mushrooms (with stems removed), soaked overnight, simmered until tender and finely sliced; keep soaking water for dashi
2 oz (60 g) salmon belly, cut into small cubes
3 green onions (scallions), white only, toasted over an open flame if possible

combine eggs, dashi, mirin and shoyu in a bowl
whisk together thoroughly
skim off any scum from the surface
pour into 6 (3-fl-oz/85-ml) Chinese teacups
put in ginkgo, shiitake, salmon and green onions
steam 10 to 12 minutes
take out of the steamer
cool for 10 to 15 minutes so they can be held easily before serving

COLD TORTILLA WITH SNAKE BEANS, OLIVES AND CAPERS

Tortilla, the Spanish name for this egg dish, is known as frittata in Italy, where it usually includes cheese. Use other vegetables in season. It makes a good lunch and can be eaten hot or cold.

Serves 6
Season: spring/summer

1 large potato, peeled and diced
4½ teaspoons olive oil
2 onions, diced
½ lb snake beans, finely sliced
2 tablespoons capers, drained
½ cup (2½ oz/75 g) pitted black olives
8 organic free-range eggs
1 teaspoon sea salt
¼ teaspoon freshly ground black pepper

boil the potatoes until just tender
drain and set aside
heat a pan and add the oil
sauté the onions until soft and browned; set aside to cool
blanch the snake beans in boiling water
refresh in cold water and set aside
preheat the oven to 335°F (170°C)
combine the potatoes, onions and snake beans with the capers and olives
whisk the eggs with the salt and pepper
pour the eggs into a greased baking dish
add the potato mixture and distribute evenly
bake, uncovered, for approximately 25 minutes or until golden brown and set
cool completely before removing from the dish
serve thick slices with a green salad and dressing

SOFT-BOILED QUAIL EGGS WITH SUGAR-CURED SALMON

If you are having a party, buy a whole salmon and have it filleted. Use half for the party and sugar-cure the rest for later use (make stock from the head and bones). Once cured, this will keep for 3 months in the freezer. Defrost overnight, in the fridge.

Serves 4 to 6
Season: summer

SUGAR-CURED SALMON
1 lb 3 oz (300 g) salmon fillet, skin on
5 teaspoons coarse sea salt
5 teaspoons grated palm sugar
½ teaspoon coarsely ground black pepper
1 bunch cilantro (coriander), roughly chopped

QUAIL EGG SALAD
1 teaspoon sea salt
1 tablespoon brown rice vinegar
2 Lebanese cucumbers, finely sliced on the diagonal
12 quail eggs
water to boil eggs
2 bunches small arugula (rocket), leaves only
extra-virgin olive oil for drizzling

to sugar-cure the salmon, place the fish, skin side down, on a large flat plate
combine the salt, sugar, pepper and cilantro
firmly pat the salt mixture over the surface of the fish
cover with a piece of cheesecloth or a fine-woven dish towel
leave in the refrigerator for 24 to 36 hours
remove the salt mixture and discard
wipe the fish
refrigerate until ready to use, or freeze for future use
to make the quail egg salad, rub the salt and vinegar into the cucumber and **set** aside
boil the eggs for approximately 3 minutes
plunge into cold water and crack the shell at one end
using a very sharp knife, slice the salmon flesh as thin as you can
serve the eggs in their shells with slices of salmon, the cucumber and arugula
drizzle extra-virgin olive oil over the leaves
provide an empty bowl for the peelings

BAKED EGGS DADDY

The daddy was mine and this was a breakfast we asked him for often, though as I recall we only got it when spinach was bountiful in Mum's vegetable garden. I once made this dish for forty in a huge baking dish – it looked wild. Use ramekin dishes if you have them: they present well and are made for the job.

Serves 6
Season: autumn/winter

1 tablespoon olive oil
1 bunch English spinach, washed
½ teaspoon sea salt
6 pats of butter
grated nutmeg to taste
¼ teaspoon freshly ground black pepper
6 organic free-range eggs
½ cup (1⅓ oz/40 g) grated Parmesan cheese

preheat oven to 400°F (200°C)
heat the oil in a large pan
add the spinach and salt
cover the pan and cook over low heat for 8 minutes
remove the lid and cook until almost no liquid remains
drain spinach, finely chop and allow to cool
butter 6 ramekin dishes
sprinkle each one with nutmeg and pepper
divide the spinach between the ramekins
make a well in the spinach
crack an egg into each well
sprinkle a little cheese on top
bake for 10 to 15 minutes

They are cooked when they rise a little and are firm. Be careful not to overcook or you will be eating India rubber.

SEAFOOD

Green tea noodles and rosemary with baby octopus

A whole fish, well presented and accompanied by a range of grain and vegetable dishes, turns a meal into an event. Many people are afraid of cooking fish, thinking that it's "too easy to produce something tough and dry." I find the main elements to consider for excellent results are: freshness, temperature when storing and cooking, and the length of time stored and cooked. Cooked quickly at a high temperature, and carefully handled, most varieties will be moist and full of flavor.

I often go to the Sydney fish markets to buy my fish. It is an immensely enjoyable event; there's a huge choice and it's often cheaper. I trust the freshness of the fish from the market. I do buy in other places but only those I know and trust, or on the recommendation of foody friends.

I seldom go to the markets with a preconception of the fish I want. I let the quality of the fish on the day dictate my choice. I buy the best-looking fish I can find and allow it to tell me what's for dinner. Inspiration floods in as I stand before a gleaming mound of just-caught beauties, whatever they are.

A tip when going to a fresh fish market: wear sensible shoes with nonslip nonporous soles. I learned this from bitter experience on early visits when I returned home with cold, wet and smelly shoes and feet.

Dear Willem,

Here is a recipe that will have your beloved swooning at the table, and if it weren't you, you probably wouldn't make it through dinner, but since I know your love of food is as great as mine I feel sure you will be there until the last little snip of noodle has been sucked up. Do try it. I want to know if it is really as good as I believe and I can't think of anyone better to try it out on. It's my very favorite sort of food – easy to make, sensuous in the process of mixing, it smells divine while it cooks and it's lusciously slippery. The flavors fill every taste bud and one leaves the table feeling replete and very sexy. Now that I'm sure you want it too, this is what to do.

Get up early before the little birdies, dress warmly, wear nonporous shoes with a nonslip sole – you are going to the fish markets! Hurry to the street, before all the best little tight, white baby octopus have had a chance to fall into some thin unemotional sushi chef's hands. Pick the tightest whitest babies and spare not a thought for their large, intelligent, but creepy mothers. Now as you leave the markets go via the aforementioned Japanese gentleman's shop and buy a packet of green tea noodles, the ones in the silver bag with green writing, that likely says "Ichi ban kan soba shop noodles." I think they are the very nicest, and you know me I've tried them all, well, most I'm sure.

Go home via Darlinghurst, stop at Chinatown on the way, and buy a huge bunch of fresh rosemary. I assume you have a big bottle of the best virgin's oil of olives and enough umeboshi vinegar to brighten up a gloomy Thursday, garlic enough to cover your foot and about as much time as it would take you and I to drink a bottle of that beautiful Margaret River white whilst we pull the week apart, and sort out who will cover what in the coming seven days. Have coffee and read the paper, cruise and enjoy the day, pick up some fresh leaves later on and head home to cook up a storm, for two or twenty. If it's appropriate invite me too.

Use the slappap pot, heat it slowly and in it place garlic and some sprigs of rosemary. Wipe it gently with a smattering of the virgin's brew and then put the cleaned octakitty in it with a heavy lid and a low flame. Leave it for one and a half hours to gently soften and cook to the texture of earlobes warmed by an open fire or railway sleepers that have burned to glowing embers but have retained their form.

Do you remember how to clean them? Cut below their eyes, push the beak through the tight hole; we have made enough comments on this for many lifetimes, just do it. Now cut through the head to extract the gushy innards. Cut above the eyes now and you will have eight legs intact and a flat piece that once cooked will roll up into a tube. Once they are cooked, strain off the juice they have made, put it in a bowl in the fridge; it will become lovely red jelly to add to the dish later on. Discard the garlic and herbs and put the wee darlings under a clean dish towel to cool. Although this will be a cold dish, I prefer my legs at room temperature, how about you?

Boil much water, add no salt or lid, cook as many noodles as you can eat and remember to give them a shock once or twice so they will be evenly cooked and tender throughout. Drain these and wash, wash, wash, cold clear water, run your hand through the noodles until they feel slippery and silky and you can't tell if your hand is amongst them or not, then they are ready. Drain very well so no water remains. In your glass blender blend lots of virgins, plenty of ume vinegar, masses of garlic and plenty of rosemary – de-sprig first or forever pick it from your teeth! If you want to cause a great sensation put all the ingredients in the fridge for an hour before blending and add the jelly too. This will make pink mayonnaise, very fru fru and impressive. Now combine the noodles and the dressing with the octopus, mix really well and leave to infuse as long as you have left. Make a big green leafy affair and, I suggest, undressing! Enjoy, my foody friend, with love.

Holly xx

LEATHER JACKET NORI ROLLS WITH UMEBOSHI SAUCE

Makes 16 pieces
Season: spring/summer

3 medium leather jacket or other firm, white-fleshed fish, steamed
2 tablespoons hulled tahini
2 tablespoons stock
1 tablespoon umeboshi paste
½ bunch each garlic chives and cilantro (coriander), finely chopped
2 sheets toasted nori

allow fish to cool and remove bones
place fish in a bowl
in a separate bowl, gently mix together tahini, stock, umeboshi paste and herbs
combine the fish with $^2/_3$ of the sauce and set aside remaining sauce
spread fish mixture on each sheet of nori and roll up
leave in the fridge for 10 to 20 minutes, covered by a clean, dry cloth
cut into bite-sized pieces and serve with a dab of the reserved umeboshi sauce and a crunchy green salad

WHOLE FISH STEAMED IN THE TRADITIONAL CHINESE MANNER

In China each fish has its own recipe; this is the one used for bream and snapper. It is excellent accompanied by a selection of Chinese greens.

Serves 6
Season: all

1 ¼-in (3-cm) fresh ginger, cut into long thin strips
½ bunch green onions (scallions), very finely sliced diagonally
6 small bream, snapper or other firm, white-fleshed fish, scaled, gutted and washed
2 tablespoons toasted sesame oil
2 tablespoons tamari

combine the ginger and green onions and set aside
steam the fish for approximately 7 minutes
place the fish on a large serving dish
sprinkle the green onions and ginger over the fish
heat the oil slowly until it is very hot
pour the hot oil over the fish (it should sizzle and release the flavors from the aromatic ginger and green onions)
sprinkle the tamari over the fish
serve immediately with rice

BLACK MUSSELS IN ANISEED BROTH

Serves 6
Season: when mussels are available

4 lb (2 kg) black mussels
2 tablespoons olive oil
2 onions, diced
6 large cloves garlic, chopped
2 leeks, diced
3 tablespoons (1½ fl oz/50 ml) Pernod
1½ cups (12 fl oz/400 ml) strong fish or vegetable stock
5 tablespoons heavy cream (optional)
freshly ground black pepper to taste

wash the mussels and remove beards
discard any mussels that do not close when picked up
heat a large pan that has a well-fitting lid

add the oil
sauté the onions until soft and translucent
add the garlic and cook for 5 minutes
stir in the leeks and cook for a further 5 minutes
pour in the Pernod and the stock
bring to the boil
add the mussels and cover the pan
stir after 2 minutes, then replace the lid
cook another 5 minutes
all the mussels should now be open
discard any that remain closed
pour in the cream if you choose to use it, and stir gently
grind some fresh pepper over the mussels and serve hot

FRESH RICE NOODLES WITH CILANTRO, SCALLOPS AND LIME PICKLE

Serves 4 to 6
Season: spring/summer

3 tablespoons peanut oil
1-in (2.5-cm) fresh ginger, finely chopped
1 bunch cilantro (coriander), leaves left whole, stems finely chopped
18 fresh scallops with corals
2 lb (1 kg) fresh rice noodles, cut into 2-in (5-cm) strips
3 tablespoons shoyu
3 tablespoons stock or water
¼ pickled lime, chopped into very fine slices
juice of 1 lime
½ bunch garlic chives, chopped into 2-in (5-cm) lengths

heat a large frying pan over high heat
add half the oil
sear the ginger and cilantro stems
stir and add the scallops
cook gently for 1 minute
remove from the pan and set aside
reheat the frying pan
add the remaining oil
add the noodles and allow them to sizzle without moving them
turn them over using a flat ᵗᵘˡᵃ once they begin to crisp at
combine the shoyu, stock
pickle and lime juice
add this and the garlic c
noodles and cook 2 min
add the scallop and gin
stir in the cilantro leav

SEARED TUNA WITH WASABI

Serves 6
Season: all

½ large daikon, finely shredded on a mandolin if you have one, or cut by hand
into very fine julienne
½ teaspoon fine sea salt
1 teaspoon ginger juice
1 tablespoon wasabi powder
1 lb (500 g) sugar snap peas
2 tablespoons apple juice concentrate
2 tablespoons mirin
1 tablespoon tamari
2 tablespoons water
2 tablespoons olive oil
6 (6½ oz/200 g) tuna steaks

combine the daikon with the sea salt and ginger juice
rub this mixture together until the daikon begins to soften; set aside
mix the wasabi powder with a small amount of boiling water to form a thick paste
shape this into a small dome
press the dome inside a small bowl
turn upside down and leave until ready to use
steam the sugar snap peas until just tender, set aside
combine the apple juice concentrate with the mirin, tamari and water
mix well and set aside
heat a heavy frying pan
add the olive oil
just before it begins to smoke, place the tuna steaks in the pan
cook on one side only, until you can see the fish change color half way up the steaks
this will take 2 to 4 minutes, depending on the thickness of the steaks
pour in the apple juice mixture and cover the pan
cook for 1 minute only
remove steaks from the pan
mix the daikon and sugar snap peas together
place a mound of this on each plate
place a small mound of wasabi on the side of each plate
put the tuna steak on the vegetables and serve while still warm
drizzle with the liquid that remains from cooking the fish

GREEN TEA NOODLES AND ROSEMARY
WITH BABY OCTOPUS

Serves 8
Season: spring/summer

olive oil
2 tablespoons fresh rosemary, leaves only
8 cloves garlic, peeled
11 oz (350 g) baby octopus, cleaned (page 23)
1 egg yolk
4 tablespoons umeboshi vinegar
3/4 cup plus 2 tablespoons (7 fl oz/200 ml) olive oil
11 oz (350 g) green tea noodles (o cha soba)
8 rosemary sprigs

brush a heavy pan with a tight-fitting lid with a little olive oil
add half the rosemary, 4 cloves garlic cut in half and the octopus
cover and place over very low heat
cook, covered, for 1½ hours or until the octopus are red and very tender; set aside
strain the liquid in the pan into a bowl and refrigerate
this liquid will become a delicious pink jelly once cold
discard the garlic and rosemary
blend the rest of the garlic and rosemary with the egg yolk and vinegar
add the reserved pink jelly
add the oil, a few drops at a time, to produce a thick pink mayonnaise; set aside
boil a large pan of water
add the noodles and stir with a fork to make sure they are separate
pour a cup of cold water into the pan once it boils vigorously
repeat this twice to ensure evenly cooked noodles
once cooked, strain and rinse under cold running water
drain well
now combine the octopus with the noodles
gently mix together with half the mayonnaise
serve in a glass bowl with extra mayonnaise and a sprig of rosemary

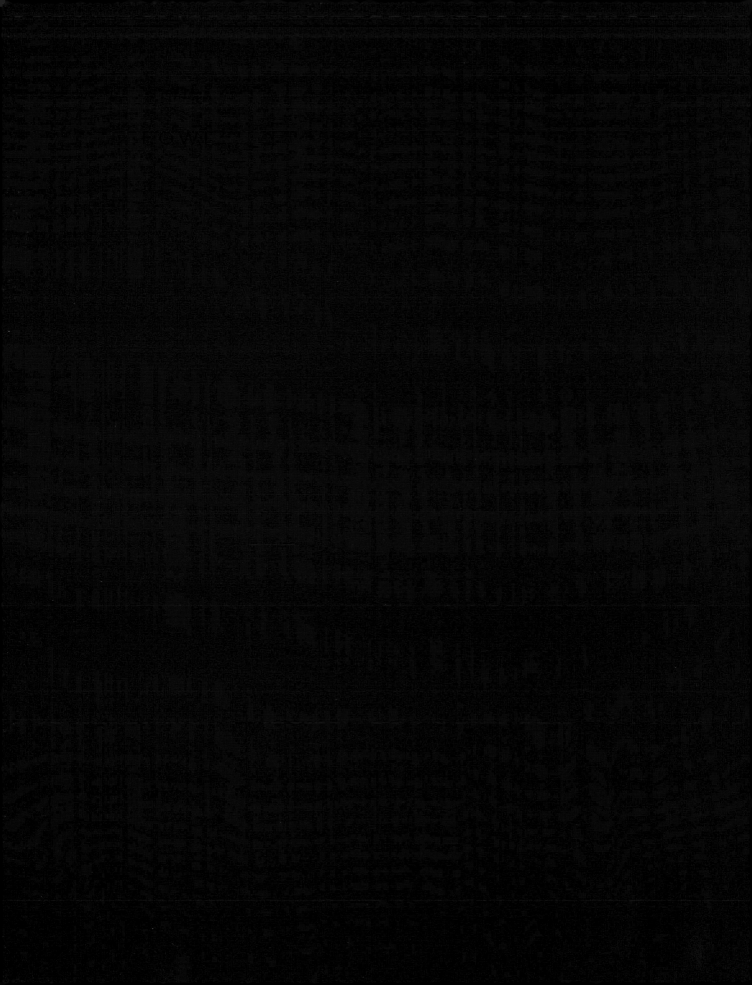

I like this name for feathered creatures that run about, and I like to know that the animals I will consume have been well treated, fed on high-quality organic grain and killed in the most humane way possible.

The pale flesh of fowl lends itself to gentle cooking, unless of course you feel like taking on the deep-fried recipe. Both result in sweet, tender and moist flesh. In spring, the activity of the liver and gall bladder, which are the organs associated with the digestion of fats, are at their peak. If you want to eat deep-fried foods this is the best time to do so. Hence the name I have given to the first recipe, the spring chicken.

I recommend serving fowl with grain or noodles, salads and lots of green vegetables so the flesh is not the predominant item on the plate. In this way it's easier to digest and you leave the table satisfied but not too heavy.

Game birds are considered fairly exotic and difficult to cook as (with the exception of duck) they have very little fat. And if they are wild, they usually have well-developed muscle which can result in dry, tough meat. The recipes given here for pheasant and duck are not difficult to make, particularly if your butcher is willing to do the jointing for you. I recommend chicken in these recipes as regular fare as game birds are more suitable for festive occasions.

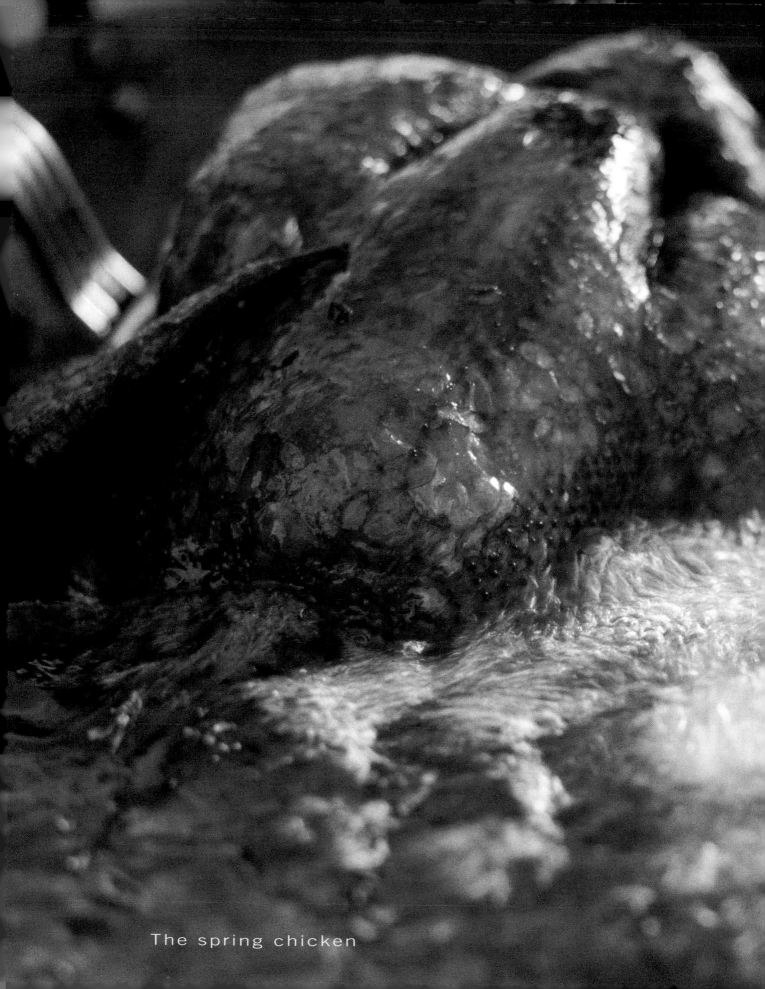

The spring chicken

THE SPRING CHICKEN

Serves 6
Season: spring

MARINADE FOR CHICKEN
1 fresh garlic bulb with green intact or ½ small leek, finely chopped
1 teaspoon sea salt
1 tablespoon shoyu
2 tablespoons Chinese rice wine (chiew)
2½ lb (1.4 kg) organic free-range chicken, well cleaned
6 cups (1.5 L) peanut oil for deep-frying

AS ACCOMPANIMENT
9½ oz (300 g) baby carrots, sliced into very fine matchsticks or
9½ oz (300 g) Lebanese cucumber, sliced in thin half moons
½ teaspoon sea salt
2 tablespoons lemon juice

SAUCE FOR CHICKEN AND RICE
1 clove garlic, very finely chopped
1-in (2.5-cm) fresh ginger, very finely chopped
3 tablespoons shoyu
5 drops chile oil
1 tablespoon toasted sesame oil
2 tablespoons black vinegar
1 tablespoon sucanat (dried sugar cane juice)
2 tablespoons chicken stock

combine the garlic or leek, salt, shoyu and rice wine in a large bowl
dry the chicken
place it in the garlic mixture and turn every 10 minutes for 40 minutes
dry carefully inside and out
heat the oil slowly
carefully immerse the chicken in the hot oil using a slotted spoon
fry to a dark red color for 10 to 15 minutes
remove from the oil and drain very well on paper
allow to rest for 10 minutes
cut into small portions on the bone using a cleaver
mix the carrots or cucumbers with the salt and lemon juice
combine all the sauce ingredients
serve the chicken with red rice (page 52) and carrots or cucumbers
drizzle the sauce over before serving

TURKEY WITH KUMQUAT PRESERVES

This is a recipe for traditional hot roast turkey. Serve slices of leftover turkey cold with kumquat preserves, plenty of fresh vegetables and a crunchy salad.

Serves as many as you have turkey for
Season: all

10 lb (5 kg) turkey, free range and organic if possible
5 tablespoons olive oil
2 teaspoons coarse sea salt
½ teaspoon coarsely ground black pepper
juice of 1 lemon
1 tablespoon chopped fresh thyme or rosemary

preheat the oven to 500°F (250°C)
clean the turkey, rinse and dry well
rub the oil, salt, pepper, lemon juice and herb into the skin and on the inside of the turkey
place uncovered in a roasting pan
roast, uncovered, for 30 minutes
cover with aluminium foil
reduce heat to 350°F (180°C)
bake for approximately 15 minutes per 1 lb (500 kg)
baste every 30 minutes with the dripping in the tray
the turkey is cooked when the juices run clear from the breast when pierced, and the leg moves easily. It is preferable to slightly undercook rather than overcook the meat
remove from the oven and leave covered for 15 minutes before serving

KUMQUAT PRESERVES
40 firm, unblemished kumquats
the same weight of grated palm sugar

wash, drain and dry the kumquats
slice thickly and remove all the seeds
place in a heavy-based stainless steel pan
add the palm sugar
cook, stirring, over low heat until the sugar has completely dissolved
cook the kumquats until their skin is translucent
pour the mixture into a hot sterile glass jar
cover with waxed paper and an airtight lid

HAINAN CHICKEN

Serves 4 to 6
Season: autumn/winter

5 quarts (20 cups/5 L) vegetable or chicken stock (pages 44 and 46)
2 teaspoons sea salt
1 (3-lb/1.5 kg) organic free-range chicken
2 cups (14 oz/440 g) biodynamic white rice
2 bunches broccoli rabe, cut hard ends off stems, then
cut so you have stems and leaves
salted ginger and sesame condiment (page 166)
1 bunch fresh cilantro (coriander), pinched into sprigs

bring stock to a boil in a large pan
add salt
remove offal and any large pieces of fat from chicken
rinse chicken in cold running water
place chicken carefully in boiling stock
return pan to a vigorous boil
turn off heat and cover pan with a well-fitting lid
leave for 2 hours
remove chicken from the pan
allow to cool enough to handle
remove all the meat from the bones in large pieces
place meat on a serving dish
put all bones and skin back into the stock
bring stock to a simmer
cook 20 to 30 minutes
strain the stock and return it to the rinsed-out pan
bring stock to a boil
remove 4 cups (1 L) of stock to cook the rice
cook rice in 4 cups stock until all the stock has been absorbed (page 50)
before serving, reheat remaining stock and blanch the broccoli rabe until tender
steam the chicken for 5 minutes to reheat
serve chicken with rice, broccoli rabe, salted ginger and sesame condiment,
cilantro sprigs and a small bowl of the chicken stock

Do make quite sure that the stock comes to a boil once you have added the bird.
This ensures any surface bacteria are killed before you turn off the stock.

ONE THOUSAND CLOVES OF GARLIC CHICKEN
BAKED ON AN OPEN FIRE

I have made this in the fire at home with great success. The trick is to have a well-built fire that has developed enough coals to simmer the pot slowly. The aim is a gentle, not a roaring, flame or the chicken will be cooked to cinders.

Serves 6
Season: winter

1 large organic free-range chicken, well cleaned
20 cloves garlic, peeled and cut in half
½ bunch thyme, leaves only
½ teaspoon sea salt
2 tablespoons olive oil
2 red onions, cut into quarters
1 large leek, cut into medium chunks
8 large whole mushrooms
5 cups (1.25 L) stock
2 tablespoons tamari

build a good fire and allow it to burn down, creating plenty of coals
rub the chicken inside and out with the garlic, thyme and salt
add the oil to a heavy pan with a well-fitting lid and handles that won't melt
place chicken, garlic and vegetables in the pan
rake the coals flat so there are no flames where the pan will sit
place the pan among the coals with the lid off
turn the contents in oil with a long-handled spoon, to seal the chicken and garlic
after about 8 minutes, add the stock and tamari
cover the pan
check the fire regularly and turn the pan to make sure it's evenly heated
bake for approximately 1 hour
serve with fresh warm bread, mashed potatoes or grains

This dish can be baked in a hot oven 400°F (200°C) when an open fire is unavailable or impractical. Follow the steps above, but seal the ingredients over a flame on top of the stove before adding the stock and placing in the preheated oven.

DUCK AND LEMON SOUP

Serves 6
Season: autumn/winter

3½ lb (1.8 kg) duck (ask the butcher to joint and return the carcass to you)
1 large leek, cut into fine matchsticks
1¼-in (3-cm) fresh ginger, cut into fine strips
1 large carrot, cut into fine matchsticks
½ large daikon, cut into fine matchsticks
8 cups (2 L) duck stock (page 47)
4 cups (1 L) strong vegetable stock (page 44)
3 tablespoons lemon juice
4 tablespoons shoyu
2 tablespoons Chinese rice wine (chiew)
6½ oz (200 g) fresh chestnuts, peeled and blanched to remove their brown skin
3½ oz (100 g) whole almonds, lightly roasted
½ bunch Italian parsley, finely chopped

heat a deep, heavy frying pan
place the duck pieces, skin side down, in the frying pan
fry for 6 minutes on each side
remove the breast pieces
continue to cook the legs for a further 5 minutes
remove the duck to a warm plate and cover with another plate
slice the breasts into 6 pieces
chop the legs and thighs in 3 pieces each, using a cleaver
return to the plate and cover
return the frying pan to the heat
pour off excess fat, leaving 2 tablespoons only (or use peanut oil)
sauté the leek until bright green
add the ginger and cook for 5 minutes
stir in the carrot and daikon and cook for 5 minutes
pour in the stocks, the seasonings and rice wine
add the chestnuts and almonds and bring to a gentle simmer
drop in the leg pieces
cook for 5 minutes
add the breast pieces
cook for 3 minutes
serve immediately topped with chopped parsley

PHEASANT AND PRESERVED LEMON CASSEROLE ON A BED OF STEAMED ALMOND COUSCOUS

Serves 6
Season: autumn/winter

2 tablespoons duck fat or peanut oil
4 lb (2 kg) pheasant or 3½ lb (1.6 kg) organic free-range chicken (ask your butcher to joint it and use the carcass to make a stock)
7 golden shallots, peeled and cut in half
1 lb (500 g) baby eggplant, cut in half lengthways and sprinkled with ½ teaspoon sea salt
8 oz (250 g) roasted tomatoes (page 54)
½ preserved lemon, finely sliced
4 oz (125 g) black olives
½ cup (4 fl oz/125 ml) verjuice or ¼ cup (2 fl oz/60 ml) good-quality white wine vinegar
1 cup (8 fl oz/250 ml) chicken stock

STEAMED ALMOND COUSCOUS
3½ cups (28 fl oz/875 ml) vegetable stock
½ teaspoon sea salt
4 oz (125 g) whole almonds, lightly roasted and finely ground
2 cups (11 oz/360 g) couscous

heat a large, deep frying pan
add the duck fat or peanut oil
quickly seal the pheasant on both sides
remove and set aside between two warm plates
in the same pan add the golden shallots
cook until beginning to brown
add the eggplant and brown on both sides
add the roasted tomatoes, preserved lemon and olives
pour in the verjuice or vinegar and the chicken stock and stir gently
pour half of this mixture into a deep oven dish
place the pheasant pieces in the dish
pour the remaining vegetable mixture on top and cover
bake in a 325°F (160°C) oven for 1 hour
to make the almond couscous, combine the stock and salt in a small pan
bring to a simmer
whisk in the almond meal and the couscous
cover and simmer for 1 minute
turn the heat off
leave covered for 20 minutes
fluff up with a fork and serve hot under the casserole

Tofu is soybean curd containing easily digested protein, B vitamins, and minerals including calcium, phosphorus, sodium, potassium and iron.

Tofu was first made in China several thousand years ago when the highly prized soybean was processed to improve its digestibility.

Tofu is made more or less warming according to the method of cooking and the ingredients it is combined with.

Tempeh is an Indonesian savory fermented soybean product made from cooked soybeans and the culture *Rhizopus oligosporus* that grows a white mold around the beans similar to the mold on Camembert cheese.

High in protein, tempeh is delicious when cut in small pieces and pan or deep-fried. It is suitable for most Asian dishes.

You may notice small black specks in the tempeh you buy; this is quite normal and does not indicate deterioration of the product.

Seitan is a Japanese recipe for wheat gluten cooked with kombu, shoyu, ginger and mirin. It is low in calories and high in protein and adds a hearty texture and flavor to stews and soups or, pan-fried, makes a great snack or sandwich filling.

MISO SOY CHEESE

Spread the tofu cheese as you might spread any soft cheese, it has a creamy texture. Or blend it with a little lemon juice, garlic and olive oil for a fantastic sauce to use over cooked vegetables, pasta, noodles or grains. Bake it in a hot oven until it sets to a golden brown. This is strong food and should be used sparingly.

Makes 12 oz (400 g)
Season: autumn/winter

12 oz (400 g) firm tofu
3 cups brown rice (gen mai) miso

place the tofu on a dish towel under a heavy chopping board to press out some of the excess moisture
dry the tofu thoroughly
spread the miso evenly all over the tofu
place the tofu on a clean dry plate

cover the tofu with a piece of cheesecloth or a clean, dry dish towel
leave at room temperature for 2 to 4 days (longer=stronger)
carefully scrape the miso off the tofu
keep this miso to use in soups or sauces
refrigerate the tofu cheese until you are ready to use it

SILKEN TOFU WITH GARLIC CHIVES AND GINGER

Serves 6
Season: summer

2 (9½ oz/300 g) blocks silken tofu, drained carefully and cut into 6 pieces
1 bunch garlic chives, finely sliced
1-in (2.5-cm) fresh ginger, finely grated
zest of 2 mandarin oranges
1 sheet toasted nori, cut into very fine strips

SAUCE
juice of 2 mandarin oranges
3 tablespoons mandarin tamari
1 tablespoon mirin
3 drops orange oil
chile oil to taste (optional)

place 1 piece of cold tofu on each plate
arrange the chives, ginger and mandarin zest in the center of each piece of tofu
combine all the sauce ingredients
drizzle a small amount of the sauce over each serving
top with crisp nori strips and serve immediately

This is a cooling dish on a hot, dry day.

THAI-STYLE TEMPEH CURRY

Vary the vegetables: use green beans in place of the bok choy or serve with sugar snap peas.

Serves 6
Season: all

peanut oil to deep-fry tempeh
8 oz (250 g) raw tempeh, cut into small triangles
3 tablespoons peanut oil
2 large onions, cut into wedges
½ bunch fresh cilantro (coriander) stems
1 lb 3 oz (600 g) kabocha pumpkin, cut into medium wedges
2 teaspoons green curry paste, or to your taste
2 tablespoons tamarind paste
1¾ cups (12 fl oz/400 ml) coconut milk
1¾ cups (12 fl oz/400 ml) Asian vegetable stock (page 46)
2 tablespoons grated palm sugar
6½ oz (200 g) bok choy stems
1 bunch fresh cilantro (coriander) leaves, roughly chopped
2 lemons, cut into generous wedges

heat the oil for frying
deep-fry the tempeh to a golden brown
drain well and set aside
heat a large pan
add 3 tablespoons oil
sauté the onions until they begin to brown
add the cilantro stems and cook 5 minutes
place the pumpkin in the pan
coat with the oil and onion mixture
gently stir in the tempeh
add the curry paste and cook 5 minutes, stirring often
add the tamarind paste, coconut milk, stock and palm sugar
bring to a simmer
cook, uncovered, until the pumpkin is almost tender
add the bok choy
simmer to thicken, reducing the liquid by half
serve on rice noodles, or brown or white rice
place plenty of cilantro on top
give each person a couple of lemon wedges to squeeze over curry before eating

JOHN DOWNES' TEMPEH TEMPLE BALLS

John has been a pioneer of new thinking and eating around whole foods in Australia. His bakeries have popularized sourdough breads in the Eastern States and Perth.

Serves 6
Season: spring/summer

1½ cups (9½ oz/300 g) glutinous white rice, soaked covered in water 6 to 8 hours
1½ cups (12 fl oz/375 ml) cold water
½ teaspoon sea salt
4 cups (1 L) peanut oil for deep frying the tempeh and the rice balls
5 oz (150 g) raw tempeh cut in ½-in (1-cm) cubes
3½ oz (100 g) dried dates, pitted and chopped
1 tablespoon finely grated fresh ginger
1 teaspoon grated mandarin or orange zest
1 teaspoon freshly ground cilantro (coriander) seeds
2 tablespoons brown rice (gen mai) miso
1 cup (8 fl oz/250 ml) water
¼ teaspoon chile sauce (optional)
9½ oz (300 g) sesame seeds

place the drained rice, the measured water and the salt in a pan
bring to a rapid boil, cover, simmer gently for 30 minutes
remove from the heat and leave covered for 5 more minutes
turn the rice out of the pan and set aside to cool, covered with a dry dish towel
heat a deep pan and add the oil
deep-fry the tempeh until golden brown
remove and drain on paper towels
in a large pan, combine dates, ginger, mandarin or orange zest, cilantro, miso, water and chile sauce, if using
cover the pan and bring to the boil
simmer gently until the dates are very soft and the mixture has thickened to a paste
add the fried tempeh and combine thoroughly
marinate the tempeh for at least 1 hour
form rice into balls with clean damp hands
make a hollow in each ball
fill with plenty of the date and tempeh mixture
seal and smooth the rice with damp hands
roll balls in sesame seeds
reheat oil for deep-frying
deep-fry to a golden brown
drain on paper towels before serving hot or cold

AIRDRE GRANT'S MUSTARD AND SAUERKRAUT TEMPEH

This recipe was taught to me by Airdre Grant, a New Zealander who came to Iku from Boston, where she was studying to become the talented cook and macrobiotic counselor she now is. Her book *The Good Little Cook Book* is definitely worth adding to your collection; see bibliography for details. I have altered the recipe slightly, as I am wont to do.

Serves 5 to 6
Season: autumn/winter

oil for pan-frying
9½ oz (300 g) block plain tempeh, cut in half lengthways, then into bite-sized triangles
1 cup (9½ oz/300 g) sauerkraut
¼ large white cabbage, sliced thinly
1 large carrot, cut into thick matchsticks
2 cups (16 fl oz/500 ml) stock
3 tablespoons rice malt
2 tablespoons smooth Dijon mustard
½ teaspoon sea salt, if required (check how salty the sauerkraut is)
1 bunch chives, finely chopped

heat the oil in a frying pan
fry the tempeh until it is crisp and golden brown
remove tempeh from the oil and drain well
place tempeh, sauerkraut and vegetables in a large pan
combine the stock with the rice malt and mustard
pour this over the ingredients in the pan
taste and add salt if required
simmer, covered, over medium heat for 30 minutes
uncover and allow liquid to reduce by half
add the chives just before serving
serve with baked potatoes, noodles or roasted millet

SIMPLE SEITAN

Gluten is a protein base to which you add the flavor of the seitan ingredients to form this product, or you can create your own flavor by infusing the wheat gluten with any ingredients you wish. You can reduce the preparation time for wheat gluten by using gluten flour instead of unbleached white flour. Replacing the unbleached white flour with other wheat flour will vary the texture and flavor.

Makes 1 lb (500 g)
Season: autumn/winter

WHEAT GLUTEN
½ teaspoon sea salt
2 cups (16 fl oz/500 ml) cold water
3½ cups (1 lb/500 g) unbleached white flour

dissolve the salt in the water
gradually add the water to the flour to form a dough
knead the dough for 10 minutes until it is smooth and elastic
place the dough in a bowl in the sink
cover with cold water
continue to knead the dough under slow running water
this separates the gluten from the bran and starch
the dough will begin to fall apart; this is as it should be
once the water runs clear, form the sticky strands of gluten into a ball
break off pieces the size of a small lime
drop them into boiling water; they will grow in size
remove when they rise to the surface
this is wheat gluten

SEITAN
6 cups (1.5 L) water
4 tablespoons tamari
4 tablespoons mirin
6-in (15-cm) stick kombu
15 inches (37.5 cm) fresh ginger, finely sliced

place the gluten and other seitan ingredients in a pressure cooker or pan with a lid
bring to full-pressure or a simmer
cook, covered, for 40 minutes in pressure cooker, or 1 hour in a pan with a lid
remove the lid
continue to cook, uncovered, until the liquid has reduced by two-thirds

Refrigerate until ready to use, keeping well-covered with the liquid.

SEITAN STEW FOR COLD WINTER NIGHTS

Whenever I eat this I am reminded of the lamb stews my mother made on cold winter nights in England. This is a satisfying and warming meal that goes well with a pickled or blanched salad.

Serves 6
Season: winter

2 tablespoons sesame oil
1 onion, cut into wedges
1 lb (500 g) carrots, large roll cut
3/4 lb (12 oz/400 g) kabocha pumpkin, large irregular cut
1 lb (500 g) potatoes, diced
4-in (10-cm) stick kombu, soaked in cold water and roughly chopped
11 oz (350 g) seitan (page 144), cut into bite-sized pieces
2½ inches (6 cm) fresh ginger, finely sliced
1 cup (8 fl oz/250 ml) vegetable stock
1 tablespoon shoyu
½ teaspoon sea salt
1 tablespoon kudzu or cornstarch (cornflour), dissolved in 4 tablespoons cold water
3 large green onions (scallions)

heat a large heavy-based pan
add the oil
sauté the onions until they are transparent
add the carrots, pumpkin and potatoes; coat with oil
cook for 15 minutes, stirring often
add the kombu, seitan and ginger; cook for 5 minutes
pour in the stock, shoyu and sea salt
bring to a simmer
cook until the vegetables are quite tender and the pumpkin is beginning to break up when stirred
thicken with the kudzu or cornstarch slurry, stirring constantly
chop the green onions and add to the stew just before serving
serve with grain and greens

There are many ways to provide our friends
and loved ones with support and the offering
of food is one of them.

Party food is a means to feed friendships.
For many people, the idea of preparing food
for large numbers is daunting, difficult and
time consuming. There are several dishes that
I use for festive occasions. I call them "The
Fish Routine." These are a collection of
simple dishes that are easy to make and
present and that can be combined to suit
most people's dietary needs. I have served
this food for parties, picnics on the beach, for
birthday celebrations, weddings and
Christmas.

Food is also offered at times of special
need: there are foods that comfort, and foods
that are said to heal, such as koi-koku carp
soup for new mothers. Comfort foods are
frequently those associated with our
childhood. (For me there is no substitute for
cold toast with thickly spread fresh butter and
Marmite!)

Dairy products also have a comforting
association, probably as a result of being the
first food consumed by most of us. I use dairy
food as sparingly as possible and I have
included a recipe for a drink that I find an
excellent substitute for a milky drink when it

The Fish Routine - Lime mayonnaise

The Fish Routine – Rice, pasta and potatoes

The Fish Routine - Pickled beets

THE FISH ROUTINE FOR WEDDINGS AND OTHER MEMORABLE EVENTS

Variations on this theme are endless: use a different fish, bake the fish or barbecue it, use different vegetables in the salads, try other types of pasta, whatever you can think of really. Present this well and it makes a lovely sight, and the best thing about it is how simple each item is to make.

Serves approximately 30 at a banquet lunch, or 20 at dinner
Season: whenever there's a party

Steamed whole fish
Lime mayonnaise (page 163)
Pickled beets (page 171)
Romano beans with new potato salad (page 88)
Biodynamic white rice with marinated vegetables (page 154)
Pasta with pesto and broccoli (page 155)
Crispy leaf salad (page 155)
Crusty sesame sourdough loaf (page 64)
Ashed goat's cheese with ripe pears, figs or persimmons when in season and thin crisp crackers (page 155)

STEAMED WHOLE FISH

7 lb (3.5 kg) whole fish (salmon, trout, coral trout or any other oily fish), scaled, gutted and washed
4 cups (1 L) fish stock (page 44) or water
6 peppercorns
2 bay leaves
1 teaspoon sea salt
2-in (5-cm) fresh ginger, sliced
1 black olive
2 Lebanese cucumbers, sliced into fine rounds
¼ teaspoon sea salt

You will need a fish kettle to cook such a large fish properly. If you don't own one, rent one from a party rental company. If you entertain regularly, a fish kettle is a great investment.

wash any blood and slime from the fish (a fresh trout or salmon should be quite slimy)
remove the trivet from the fish kettle
pour in the stock or water

put the peppercorns, bay leaves, 1 teaspoon salt and the ginger in the water

cover, and put the kettle on the stove over 2 burners

bring to a boil and simmer 5 minutes

remove the lid

place the fish on the trivet and carefully lower it into the kettle

simmer, covered, approximately 20 minutes

test with a sharp knife behind the head; the fish is cooked once the flesh will just come away from the bone

lift out the trivet and carefully slide the fish onto a serving plate

serve now if serving hot or cool under a clean dish towel

take the skin off and remove the eye

place the olive in the eye socket

rub the cucumber with ¼ teaspoon sea salt

place the cucumber around the fish to serve

serve the fish hot, warm or cold

BIODYNAMIC WHITE RICE WITH MARINATED VEGETABLES

3 cups (1 lb 6 oz/660 g) short-grain biodynamic white rice

5½ cups (1.35 L) water

1 teaspoon sea salt

5 oz (150 g) sundried tomatoes, finely sliced

1½ oz (50 g) small salted capers

5 oz (150 g) Ligurian (small black) olives

6½ oz (200 g) marinated artichoke hearts, cut into quarters

1 bunch parsley, roughly chopped

sea salt

5 tablespoons (2½ fl oz/80 ml) extra-virgin olive oil

freshly ground black pepper

place the rice, water and salt together in a large pan

cover with a well-fitting lid

bring to the boil over high heat

turn very low and simmer for 35 minutes

remove the pan from the heat

do not uncover for a further 15 minutes

turn out into a large bowl to cool a little

mix all the remaining ingredients through the rice

leave for about 1 hour

serve at room temperature

PASTA WITH PESTO AND BROCCOLI

1 tablespoon sea salt
8 quarts (32 cups/8 L) boiling water
9½ oz (300 g) broccoli, cut into florets
2 lb (1 kg) pasta
2 tablespoons extra-virgin olive oil
½ teaspoon sea salt
freshly ground black pepper
4 tablespoons pesto
½ bunch basil, leaves only
4 tablespoons toasted pine nuts
fresh flakes of Parmesan cheese
(optional)

put the 1 tablespoon sea salt in the boiling water
blanch the broccoli
remove from the water, leaving it to boil
refresh the broccoli in cold water
drain well and set aside
pour the pasta into the boiling water
cook according to the instructions
drain once the pasta is al dente
immediately return the pasta to the pan
pour in the olive oil, salt and pepper
spoon the pasta into a serving dish
add the broccoli florets and mix
to serve, put dabs of pesto on the top of the pasta, arrange the basil leaves on top and sprinkle the pine nuts over
put the Parmesan cheese in a separate dish

CRISPY LEAF SALAD

3 large heads iceburg lettuce
½ teaspoon sea salt
juice of ½ lemon
1 tablespoon aged balsamic vinegar
3 tablespoons extra-virgin olive oil

wash the lettuce carefully and dry well
break into bite-sized chunks
just before serving, sprinkle with the remaining ingredients

ASHED GOAT'S CHEESE AND SELECTED FRUIT

9½ oz (300 g) ashed goat's cheese
selected fruit, washed and dried
thin crisp crackers

remove the cheese from the refrigerator at least 1 hour before serving
remove any wrapping and place the cheese on a dry board
place the fruit around the cheese with some thin crisp crackers
supply a knife for people to cut the cheese and fruit as they serve themselves

Stocking the larder in preparation for a birth

I can think of few higher honors than to be asked to assist at the birth of a friend's baby. I have twice had the privilege to be at the birth of children who will always have a special place in my heart. Both births were to be at home and my task was inevitably to take care of the food needs for the mother and the rest of the support team.

I took the role seriously, and since having a home birth of my own, I offer others who may be in this position a few useful tips. I have included a couple of "food as medicine" ideas that may also be of assistance during a long labor.

About one month prior to the birth, shop for the dry goods and store them at the home of the birthing woman, either in the larder or packed so they can be taken easily to the hospital.

My experience of hospital food has not been good so I prefer to provide my own if it is possible. If you are caring for someone in hospital, prepare yourself by having at least two good thermos flasks and several stainless steel containers with lids that seal well. I prefer stainless steel as it is easy to sterilize and it will not taint the food.

Consider who will be at the birth before shopping for food. Find out all their special needs and preferences. Consider the mother's needs and ask her what she likes to eat and drink and what her medical caregivers suggest. Small amounts of food can be offered regularly to a woman in labor; let her choose what to eat.
For the mother:
— Plenty of filtered water; a selection of herbal teas
— Lemons and honey to add to water or tea
— Mineral water and juice — apple juice is considered more appropriate than orange juice
— A variety of cereals for small meals and breakfast
— Rice, soy or cow's milk as preferred
— Plenty of fresh fruit
— Ice cubes

Make a selection of light nourishing meals that can be cooked without too much fuss, such as soft-cooked rice, wrapped in nori. Broths, light vegetable soups and miso soups are ideal. Noodles in broth are also good. Avoid sticky and oily foods. Baked potatoes, toast and spreads are good to have on hand for the support team.

A tip if you are a support person: try to eat, drink and sleep away from the woman in labor.

KOI-KOKU CARP SOUP FOR NEW MUMS

This traditional Japanese dish is usually given to a woman just after she has had a baby. It is said to be beneficial to the blood, a restorative that assists in the production of breast milk and gives strength to the new mother. Traditionally the fish guts are left in when the soup is made. I find this too earthy for my liking so I gut the fish first.

Serves 3 to 4
Season: when feeling weak or soon after giving birth

1 lb 10 oz (800 g) burdock root (gobo)
1 tablespoon corn oil
$^3/_4$ lb (12 oz/400 g) carp (koi), scaled and gutted
1 handful bancha tea twigs (in a cheesecloth bag)
1 cup barley (mugi) or brown rice (gen mai) miso
2 teaspoons grated fresh ginger
$^1/_4$ bunch green onions (scallions), finely chopped

peel the burdock and shave it with a sharp knife as you would sharpen a pencil
heat a 5-quart pan
sauté the burdock in the oil for 10 minutes
clean the carp and cut into 1-in (2.5-cm) chunks, include the head and tail
lay the fish over the burdock and cover with water to 1 in (2.5 cm) above fish
put the tea bag on top
cover and simmer for 2 to 3 hours, or pressure cook for 1$^1/_2$ hours
mix the miso with a little stock and add to the soup
simmer a further 40 minutes to 1 hour
remove the tea bag
serve pieces of fish with some of the broth, a little ginger and some green onions on top

The bancha tea is said to assist in softening the bones of the fish and to add calcium to the dish.

NANCY BYRNES' FISH SOUP

This is my adaptation of John and Nancy's joint creation. John is generally responsible for the stock and Nancy for the soup.

Serves 6
Season: whenever you like

³/₄ cup (3½ oz/100 g) finely ground brown rice flour
½ cup (4 fl oz/125 ml) olive oil
8 cups (2 L) strong, clear fish stock (page 44)
½ cup (4 fl oz/125 ml) white wine
2 tablespoons sour cream
2 tablespoons lime juice
1 teaspoon fish sauce
sea salt to taste
freshly ground black pepper to taste

heat a heavy pan and dry-roast the rice flour for a couple of minutes
add the oil and stir
vigorously whisk in the fish stock, a little at a time over medium heat
cook, stirring frequently, until the soup is thick and smooth
pour in the wine
combine the sour cream, lime juice and fish sauce to a smooth cream
stir this into the soup
season with salt and pepper
serve hot with crusty bread

CHICKEN SOUP TO CURE ALL ILLS

Serves 6 to 8
Season: autumn/winter

5 large cloves garlic
¼ lb (4 oz/125 g) carrots, roll cut
½ lb (8 oz/250 g) leeks, sliced
2 onions, diced
³/₄ cup diced celery
½ lb (8 oz/250 g) fennel, diced
9½ oz (300 g) celeriac, large diced
1 lb (500 g) potatoes, large diced
1 whole organic free-range chicken
8 cups (2 L) vegetable stock
1½ teaspoons sea salt
juice of ½ lemon
½ bunch Italian parsley, finely chopped

wash all vegetables well
place cleaned chicken and all vegetables in pan
cover with vegetable stock; add the salt
bring to a simmer
do not boil
allow to simmer 1½ to 2 hours
remove chicken; cool a little
take flesh from the bones and set flesh aside
discard the bones
bring soup back to a simmer
add the lemon juice
place meat back into soup
serve sprinkled with parsley

A CAKE FOR WEDDINGS AND CHRISTMAS

Serves approximately 50
Season: any special event

9½ oz (300 g) organic golden raisins
11 oz (350 g) organic dried figs
8 oz (250 g) organic raisins
4 oz (125 g) organic currants
3½ oz (100 g) organic dried cherries, pitted
2 teaspoons ground cinnamon
1 teaspoon grated nutmeg
½ teaspoon ground cloves
juice and grated zest of 3 large oranges
1 tablespoon white (shiro) miso
2 cups (16 fl oz/500 ml) stout beer
¼ cup plus 2 tablespoons (5 fl oz/150 ml) corn oil
4 oz (125 g) whole macadamia nuts, lightly toasted
2 cups (8 oz/250 g) whole-wheat flour
1½ cups plus 2 tablespoons (6½ oz/200 g) unbleached white flour
1 cup (8 fl oz/250 ml) leaven (page 63)

combine the first 11 ingredients and soak overnight
the following day, mix in the oil and nuts
combine half the flours, and add a little at a time; mix well
incorporate the leaven and the remaining flour
pour into a lined and well-oiled deep 9-in (22-cm) square cake pan
leave to rise, covered, in a warm spot for 6 to 8 hours
place, covered with foil, in a very low oven 200°F (100°C)
bake for 8 hours, uncover and bake a further 20 minutes at 335°F (170°C)
remove from the oven and cool on a wire rack before taking out of the pan

ROOIBOS TEA

Here is a comforting drink from my friend Nicholaas, who called it "Mother's Milk."

Makes 4 cups (1 L)
Season: all

4 cups (1 L) water
3 teaspoons rooibos tea or 3 teabags
¾ cup (6 fl oz/185 ml) soy milk
4 teaspoons raw honey

bring water to a simmer in a small pot
sprinkle in the tea leaves or teabags
simmer for 10 minutes gently
strain into 4 cups
add soy milk and honey to taste

SAUCES

Green herb dressing for salads and vegetables

A simple bowl of grains, greens or salad is made more interesting, and often more appetizing, with the addition of a sauce. Sauces add complex or subtle flavors; they vary the texture, increase the moisture and generally improve a dish.

Traditional sauces can be high in fat and need a great deal of care when making them. These recipes, on the other hand, are quick and easy to make.

I like to present sauces separately so people have the choice of if, where and how much to have. All these sauces keep well for at least ten days and I recommend making a double batch and storing them in sealed glass containers in the refrigerator.

GREEN HERB DRESSING FOR SALADS AND VEGETABLES

Serves 6
Season: all

4½ teaspoons Dijon mustard
2 tablespoons white wine vinegar
1 tablespoon finely chopped basil leaves
1 tablespoon finely chopped chives
½ bunch parsley, roughly chopped
1 clove garlic, chopped
1 tablespoon apple juice concentrate
4 tablespoons olive oil

blend in the order given
when you get to the olive oil, drizzle it in slowly to create an emulsion

UMEBOSHI AND TAHINI SAUCE

A great standby that only takes a minute to whip up. It enlivens simple fare.

Makes 11 fl oz (350 ml)
Season: all

2 teaspoons umeboshi plum paste
3 tablespoons tahini
1 tablespoon lemon juice
1½ teaspoons tamari
warm stock to mix to desired thickness

combine the umeboshi paste with the tahini, lemon juice and tamari
gradually mix in the stock, and it will thicken as the tahini absorbs the stock
when it is just pourable, stop
taste for seasoning
allow to rest before using
use in small amounts with fish or vegetables

BLACK BEAN SAUCE

Serves 6
Season: autumn/winter

3 tablespoons peanut oil
2 onions, cut in half and sliced
3 cloves garlic, chopped
1 tablespoon grated fresh ginger
1 small, hot red chile, finely chopped
2 tablespoons salted black beans, soaked in boiling water for 30 minutes then drained
6 shiitake mushrooms, with stems removed, covered in boiling water and soaked for 20 minutes, reserve mushroom liquid, drain mushrooms and finely slice
2 cups (16 fl oz/500 ml) stock, including mushroom soaking liquid
3 tablespoons mirin
3 tablespoons Chinese rice wine (chiew)
3 tablespoons shoyu
2 tablespoons kudzu or cornstarch (cornflour), dissolved in cold water

heat a pan and add the oil
sauté onions until soft and starting to brown
add the garlic, ginger, chile and black beans and cook 3 minutes
add mushroom slices, stock, mirin, Chinese rice wine and shoyu
simmer 10 minutes
thicken with kudzu or cornstarch slurry and cook 3 minutes

LIME MAYONNAISE

Serves 12
Season: all

1 organic free-range egg
2 cloves garlic
1 tablespoon umeboshi vinegar
1 tablespoon mirin
2 teaspoons lime juice
5 drops lime oil
4 tablespoons olive oil

blend first 6 ingredients in the order given
slowly add the olive oil to form an emulsion
refrigerate until ready to serve

CONDIMENTS

Deep-fried kombu bows

Condiments are designed as small dishes with strong flavors that create highlights in a meal. They add flavor, texture, color and interest.

I like to create simple meals that offer people plenty of choices. I often serve meals at home in separate serving bowls where there may be a grain dish, one or two vegetable dishes, some protein such as a bean dish or perhaps fish or chicken, and as a condiment, a pickled or boiled salad or a sea vegetable dish. This may sound like a banquet, but it is actually quite simple food, and it can usually be prepared in the time it takes to cook the grains.

Some of these condiments can also be stored in airtight containers in the refrigerator for several days; others are best made in small amounts just before serving.

SALTED GINGER AND SESAME CONDIMENT

This condiment is traditionally served with Hainan chicken (page 132) but it is also delicious with grains and vegetables.

Serves 4 to 6
Season: autumn/winter

6¼ inches (15.5 cm) fresh ginger (the younger the better)
1 bunch green onions (scallions)
1 teaspoon sea salt
1 tablespoon toasted sesame oil

dice the ginger as fine as possible
cut the green onions into very fine rounds
combine these in a glass or ceramic bowl
rub in the salt until the mixture feels wet
pour the sesame oil in and mix well
let this sit for an hour if possible or refrigerate in a glass jar for later use

GOMASHIO

This is a Japanese condiment made from hulled sesame seeds (goma) and sea salt (shio). These are dry-roasted and ground together, so that the oil from the seeds coats the sea salt, making both more easily absorbed by the body. Chewing half a teaspoon of gomashio is said to be helpful if you have a headache or are feeling vague or exhausted.

Makes as much as desired
Season: all

1 part unrefined sea salt
25 parts hulled sesame seeds, washed in a fine sieve and drained well

heat a heavy frying pan
add the sea salt and stir gently as it dries out
add the sesame seeds to the pan and stir to combine with the sea salt
stir continuously until the sesame seeds are golden brown and smell nutty
the mix is ready when a seed can be crushed easily between your thumb and little finger
pour the hot mix into a small grinding bowl (suribachi)
grind the mix using a pestle (surikogi)
when most of the seeds are crushed, the mix is ready to use
allow to cool completely before storing

SWEET SHOYU AND ARAME SEA VEGETABLE CONDIMENT

Serves 6
Season: summer

1 oz (30 g) dry arame or hijiki
1 tablespoons black vinegar
1½ teaspoons shoyu
1 tablespoon rice malt
3 drops chile oil
3½ teaspoons sesame oil
½ bunch chives cut in ¼-in (0.5-cm) lengths

soak the arame or hijiki in boiling water for 5 minutes
drain well; set aside
combine the black vinegar, shoyu, rice malt and chile oil
heat a frying pan; add the sesame oil
sauté the chives for 1 minute
add the drained arame or hijiki and cook a further 2 minutes
pour in the combined liquids
simmer gently until almost all the liquid has gone
spoon into a small dish and serve with grains and vegetables

DEEP-FRIED KOMBU BOWS

Makes 14 bows
Season: all

16-in (40-cm) stick kombu
peanut oil to deep-fry

cover the kombu with a damp cloth
this will soften it just enough to make it flexible
if it is too damp it will spit in the oil
cut with scissors into 1¼-in (3-cm) strips
cut a slit ½-in (1-cm) long in the center of each strip
push one end through the hole and half turn the strip inside out; this is the bow
dry well if needed
heat the oil
deep-fry the kombu for 40 to 60 seconds
drain well on paper towels and serve immediately for crisp chips

Small amounts of pickled vegetables eaten with fried foods and at the end of a meal can aid digestion. Pickles assist in the absorption of fats, and fermented pickles such as sauerkraut, help to promote the growth of *Lactobacillus acidophilus*, found as intestinal flora.

As pickles are very strong foods, high in salt and/or vinegar, it is wise to eat them in small amounts. Quickly made pickles are lighter and can be eaten in larger amounts as salads. But it is advisable to eat less of these than steamed, boiled or raw salads.

Just about any vegetable can be pickled but it is necessary to dry out vegetables with a high water content if you intend to pickle them for a prolonged period of time.

PICKLES

Lemon and cucumber cabbage pickles

LEMON AND CUCUMBER CABBAGE PICKLES

I prefer this with Chinese cabbage, but if it is unavailable use green or white cabbage instead. You may need to add a little extra time for these crisper cabbages to pickle.

Lebanese cucumbers are the small thin ones, sometimes called baby cucumbers or Japanese cucumbers. They have a sweet flavor and the skins are not as tough as their larger relations. As long as they are clean there is no need to peel them.

Black sesame seeds look and taste good in this pickle. Add them just before serving, as they tend to dye the cabbage an unattractive gray if prepared too long in advance.

This pickle can be prepared as a long-term pickle in a similar way to sauerkraut. As the cabbage ferments, it gets a delicious taste though it becomes rather strong smelling.

Serves 6
Season: winter

¼ large Chinese cabbage
1 Lebanese cucumber
1 teaspoon sea salt
1 tablespoon lemon juice
zest of ½ lemon
1 teaspoon wakame flakes
1 tablespoon rice vinegar
2 tablespoons black sesame seeds, lightly toasted

cut the cabbage into thin slices and place in a bowl
cut the cucumber in half lengthways, and slice into half moons
add to the cabbage
rub in the sea salt until the mixture feels wet
add the lemon juice and zest
simmer the wakame in a little water for 5 minutes
drain, keeping the liquid for stock
marinate the wakame in the rice vinegar for 5 minutes
combine the wakame and rice vinegar with the cabbage mixture
strain off any excess liquid and use for stock
sprinkle in the black sesame seeds just before serving
mix lightly

GARLIC PICKLED MUSHROOMS

It is hard to stop eating these once you have begun. They have a marvelous texture and a full, rich flavor that goes well with grains. Vary the type of mushrooms you use and try them with balsamic vinegar instead of lemon juice.

Serves 8
Season: spring/summer

½ lb (8 oz/250 g) mushrooms, stems removed
2 large cloves garlic, very finely chopped
1½ teaspoons toasted sesame oil
1 tablespoon tamari
1½ teaspoons lemon juice

slice the mushrooms thickly
place in a large bowl
add the rest of the ingredients and mix well
marinate for 30 minutes to 1 hour
drain before serving
use the liquid over rice vermicelli

This makes a great addition to a broccoli or bean salad or eat as a pickle.

PICKLED BEETS

Serves 4 to 6
Season: autumn

2 large beets (beetroot) or 12 tiny beets (beetroot)
1 teaspoon sea salt
¼ cup plus 3 tablespoons (3½ fl oz/100 ml) rice vinegar
3 tablespoons (1½ fl oz/50 ml) balsamic vinegar
2 tablespoons (1 fl oz/30 ml) olive oil

boil the beets until tender
place in cold water and when cool enough to handle, peel
chop into bite-sized pieces if using large beets
add the salt
combine with the vinegars and oil
cool in the refrigerator before serving

SWEET THINGS

Rich cocoa and walnut torte

Dutch cocoa mousse

Cashew candy with star anise and sesame

Individual coconut and mango custards

ROSEMARY LEMON SYRUP CAKES

These fragrant little cakes are ideal for morning or afternoon tea or coffee. Simply made, they cook quickly and are wonderful if eaten while still slightly warm.

Makes 12 tiny teacakes
Season: all

SYRUP
8 oz (250 g) palm sugar
2 cups (16 fl oz/500 ml) water
¼ cup plus 3 tablepsoons (3½ fl oz/100 ml) lemon juice
4 sprigs fresh or dry rosemary, leaves removed

CAKE
zest of 4 lemons
1½ oz (50 g) golden raisins
1 oz (30 g) pine nuts, lightly toasted
3½ oz (100 g) almond meal
2 cups (8 oz/250 g) unbleached white self-raising flour
3 organic free-range eggs
2½ oz (80 g) grated palm sugar
¼ cup plus 3 tablepsoons (3½ fl oz/100 ml) olive oil
½ cup (4 fl oz/120 ml) lemon juice
½ teaspoon pure vanilla extract

prheat oven to 350°F (180°C)
to make the syrup, combine all ingredients in a pan
boil for 25 minutes or until it is a thin pourable consistency; set aside
combine all the dry ingredients for the cake
blend the wet ingredients in the order given, starting with the eggs
fold wet into dry
don't overwork the mix
pour into an oiled muffin pan for 12 small muffins
bake for 30 to 40 minutes; check at 25 minutes
remove the muffin pan from the oven
brush cakes liberally with the syrup two or three times
carefully remove them from the pan
cool on a wire rack
serve with a drizzle of syrup

RICH COCOA AND WALNUT TORTE

This is perfect for those who love bitter chocolate and cakes that are rich, moist, very dark and not too sweet. Add a little brandy when blending the oranges for extra decadence. It's also good served with berries in season.

Serves 6
Season: all

4 cups (12 oz/400 g) ground walnuts
1 cup Dutch cocoa powder
½ teaspoon freshly ground cardamom seeds
½ teaspoon sea salt
1 cup (8 fl oz/250 ml) maple syrup
2 unpeeled whole oranges (navel if available), boiled and well drained, seeds removed (if navels unavailable)
5 organic free-range eggs
whipped cream (optional)

preheat oven to 335ºF (170ºC)
combine all the dry ingredients in a large bowl
blend the maple syrup and the whole oranges to create an emulsion
whisk the eggs to a foamy consistency
gently fold the wet ingredients into the dry
pour into an oiled cake pan
bake for approximately 1 hour
remove from the oven and cool completely before turning out
serve with dollops of whipped cream if you like

As this is a very moist cake, it keeps for 2 or 3 days (though once you begin eating it, it's hard to stop).

FLOURLESS ORANGE AND ALMOND CAKE

This cake is a winner with everyone who tastes it. Moist and moorish, it's not a bad idea to make two.

Serves 6 to 8
Season: whenever navel oranges are in season

1½ unpeeled whole navel oranges, boiled in water until very soft
6½ oz (200 g) silken tofu, drained
1 teaspoon orange flower water
8 oz (250 g) palm sugar, grated
½ cup (4 fl oz/125 ml) olive oil
12 oz (400 g) ground almond meal
zest of 1 lemon
zest of 2 oranges
1 teaspoon baking powder

ORANGE SYRUP
1 teaspoon orange flower water
2 cups (16 fl oz/500 ml) orange juice
8 oz (250 g) palm sugar

preheat oven to 350°F (180°C)
blend the oranges, silken tofu, orange flower water, grated palm sugar and oil until smooth; set aside
combine the almond meal, lemon and orange zest and baking powder in a large bowl
gently fold the blended ingredients into the dry ingredients; the mixture will be fairly wet
pour the batter into an oiled 9-in (22-cm) cake pan
bake, uncovered, for approximately 1 hour
check after 45 minutes and cover with foil if it is getting too dark on top
cool completely before removing from the cake pan
to make orange syrup, place all ingredients in a pan
stir, without boiling, until sugar dissolves
boil for approximately 15 minutes until syrup has thickened
pour over the cake as you serve

SILKY KUDZU SOY CUSTARD

The taste of this creamy custard relies on the soy milk you use; choose one that is smooth and not too "beany" in flavor. Vary the flavor by using different sweet spices such as cinnamon, cardamom, ginger or star anise instead of the vanilla.

Make a winter pudding by adding cooked fruit to the custard and baking it for 20 minutes in a hot oven.

Serves 6
Season: all

2 cups (16 fl oz/500 ml) soy milk
½ vanilla bean, split
¼ cup plus 3 tablespoons (3½ fl oz/100 ml) maple syrup
3 tablespoons kudzu or cornstarch (cornflour), dissolved in 6 tablespoons cold water

warm the milk
place split vanilla bean in soy milk
add maple syrup
simmer gently for 15 minutes
do not boil
remove vanilla bean
scrape the bean and place the seeds back in the milk
thicken with kudzu or cornstarch slurry
check sweetness and adjust as desired
pour into a jug and allow to cool slightly
serve hot or cold

INDIVIDUAL COCONUT AND MANGO CUSTARDS

Serves 8
Season: summer

1 lb 10 oz (800 g) fresh ripe mangoes, peeled and sliced
½ teaspoon orange flower water
5 drops orange oil
½ cup plus 2 tablespoons (5 fl oz/150 ml) water
1½ cups (12 fl oz/400 ml) coconut milk
pinch sea salt
½ cup (1½ oz/50 g) fine yellow cornmeal or rice flour

macerate the mango slices in the orange flower water and orange oil
bring the water to the boil in a small pan
whisk in the coconut milk and salt
add the cornmeal or rice flour and bring the mixture back to the boil
whisk constantly while the mixture thickens
blend half the mango slices and stir into the coconut custard mixture
pour into small bowls
refrigerate the bowls for 1 hour to allow the custards to set
turn the custards out onto small plates
arrange a few slices of the remaining mango on each plate before serving

HAZELNUT OAT CREAM WITH MAPLE SYRUP

Serves 6 to 8
Season: all

2 cups leftover cold porridge or ½ cup (3 oz/85 g) rolled oats,
cooked to a porridge
½ cup (2½ oz/80 g) hazelnuts, lightly roasted
2 teaspoons ground cinnamon
½ cup (4 fl oz/125 ml) maple syrup
1½ cups (12 fl oz/375 ml) soy milk

purée porridge in a blender
add the hazelnuts, cinnamon and maple syrup and blend
thin to desired consistency with the soy milk

If you are making this with hot porridge, it will thicken as it cools.

DELIGHTFUL GREEN TEA GEL WITH GINGERED PINEAPPLE

Matcha is best to use for a strong flavor and deep color. It is green tea ground very finely. If you use it for tea, whisk it into a froth and do not let it steep for long, as it will become bitter.

Makes 8 (2½ fl oz/80 ml) jellies
Season: autumn

2 tablespoons green tea (matcha or sencha)
1 cup (8 fl oz/250 ml) boiling water
1 cup (8 fl oz/250 ml) water
1½ teaspoons agar-agar powder
5 oz (150 g) pale palm sugar, grated
3 tablespoons kudzu or cornstarch (cornflour), dissolved in 3 tablespoons cold water

GINGERED PINEAPPLE
5 oz (150 g) palm sugar
1 tablespoon ginger juice
1 small pineapple, about 1 lb (500 g), peeled and sliced thickly

put the tea in a ceramic teapot
pour the boiling water onto the tea
allow the tea to infuse for 1 minute only
strain the tea into a cup and allow to cool
bring the second cup of water to a simmer
sprinkle in the agar-agar and whisk well
simmer for 5 minutes
add the palm sugar and whisk while it dissolves
take the pan off the heat and add the kudzu or cornstarch slurry
place back on the heat
whisk constantly while the mixture thickens and clears
turn the heat off
pour the green tea into the agar-agar mixture and whisk well
pour the mixture into molds
place in the refrigerator on a flat tray to set
carefully turn the jellies out onto flat white plates
to make gingered pineapple, heat a heavy frying pan
add the palm sugar and the ginger juice
turn up the heat and add the pineapple
reduce over high heat until the syrup is thick and beginning to brown
serve with the jellies

LEMON MYRTLE AND WATERMELON JELLY

Makes 8 (4 fl oz/125 ml) jellies
Season: summer

³/₄ cup plus 2 tablespoons (7 fl oz/200 ml) water
10 dried lemon myrtle leaves or 2 tablespoons chopped lemon balm
12 lb (6 kg) watermelon
7½ teaspoons sucanat (dried sugar cane juice) or palm sugar
4 teaspoons agar-agar powder
2 tablespoons kudzu or cornstarch (cornflour), dissolved in 2 tablespoons cold water
lemon myrtle leaves or mint leaves

boil the water and infuse the lemon myrtle leaves or lemon balm for 5 minutes to make a strong tea
set aside to cool before straining
remove the flesh from the melon
mash the flesh in a large bowl
pour this into a clean fine-woven dish towel or cheesecloth
squeeze to extract all the liquid
discard the pulp and the seeds
measure the juice; there will be about 10 cups (2.5 L)
pour the juice into a large pan
bring to a simmer, uncovered
add the sucanat or palm sugar and stir well
simmer, uncovered, until the liquid has reduced to 4 cups (1 L)
set aside to cool
remove 11 fl oz (350 ml) of the reduced juice to a small pan
simmer and sprinkle with the agar-agar powder
whisk well and simmer for 7 minutes or until the agar-agar has dissolved
thicken the agar mixture with the kudzu or cornstarch slurry
stir constantly while it thickens and clears
remove from the heat
stir it into the rest of the reduced juice with the strained tea
mix well
rinse 8 small flat-bottomed bowls in cold water
pour ¼ cup (4 fl oz/125 ml) of the liquid into each bowl
place the bowls in the refrigerator on a flat tray until set
carefully turn the jellies out of the bowls onto a flat plate
serve with lemon myrtle leaves or fresh mint leaves

To turn the lemon myrtle leaves a rusty red, simmer some extra leaves in the watermelon juice as it reduces. Remove and set aside to use as a garnish.

SQUASH AND ORANGE WAU BAUL BAUMS

I learned a lot about food from the talented chef, Mindy Byrne. She popularized this name for a wobbly jelly when she had the dining room at the Palisade Hotel in The Rocks in Sydney in the early 1980s. When customers would inquire as to what a wau baul baum was the answer came, "it's a bit like a ba var ois" or, "it's German for wobblebum." I have taken the name on as these jellies are particularly colorful, and deserve to be treated as fun food.

Try adding some ginger – it spices them up no end.

Makes 10 small (5 fl oz/150 ml) molds
Season: autumn/winter

1 lb 10 oz (800 g) peeled butternut squash, cut into medium dice
4½ teaspoons agar-agar flakes
1 cup (8 fl oz/250 ml) water
1½ cups plus 2 tablespoons (5 fl oz/150 ml) maple syrup
1½ cups plus 2 tablespoons (5 fl oz/150 ml) fresh orange juice
1 tablespoon lemon juice
2 teaspoons kudzu or cornstarch (cornflour), dissolved in 2 tablespoons cold water
zest of 2 oranges
zest of 1 lemon
3½ oz (100 g) fresh roasted almonds, cooled and chopped roughly

steam squash and set aside
combine agar-agar and water
bring to a simmer and cook until agar-agar has dissolved
pour in the maple syrup and orange and lemon juice
whisk together well
heat until simmering
whisk in the kudzu or cornstarch slurry
stir constantly until mixture clears and thickens
purée squash adding a little of the orange mixture at a time
incorporate the rest of the orange mixture until smooth
add the orange and lemon zest
do a test set (page 27) before adding the almonds
set in individual molds and leave in the refrigerator until ready to serve

DUTCH COCOA MOUSSE

These are suprisingly similar to my Mum's rum and cocoa mousse though they contain no cream, eggs, or rum! They set to a soft gel and are served in small cups to be eaten with a teaspoon.

Make certain the rice flour is fully cooked or the texture will be a little gritty.

Serves 6
Season: all

½ cup (2½ oz/80 g) rice flour
2 cups (16 fl oz/500 ml) soy milk
1 tablespoon agar-agar flakes, simmered until dissolved in ½ cup plus 2 tablespoons (5 fl oz/150 ml) water; keep warm
4 tablespoons Dutch cocoa powder
½ cup (4 fl oz/125 ml) carob molasses
1 teaspoon orange flower water
2 drops orange oil
½ teaspoon vanilla extract

put the flour in a pan
whisk in the soy milk
slowly bring to a simmer, whisking constantly
cook for approximately 15 minutes or until rice flour turns from grainy to glossy
add the warm agar-agar mixture and stir well to combine
separately combine the cocoa, carob molasses, orange flower water, orange oil and vanilla to form a smooth paste
pour the cocoa mixture into the custard and whisk vigorously over low heat
pour into little bowls or mousse pots and refrigerate until ready to serve

CASHEW CANDY WITH STAR ANISE AND SESAME

Perhaps this would be better named stickjaw. It is certainly unsuitable for those with loose teeth or fillings. Try using other roasted nuts or seeds, leave out the sesame seeds or add lemon zest and cinnamon instead of star anise.

Makes 20+
Season: when you need something sweet and chewy

1 lb (500 g) jar maltose syrup
2 points star anise
3½ oz (100 g) lightly roasted cashew nuts, roughly chopped
5 oz (100 g) lightly roasted sesame seeds

stand the jar of maltose syrup in hot water for 10 minutes to soften
pour syrup into a heavy-based pan
add star anise
bring to a boil
simmer until it has reduced by one-third
fold in the nuts and seeds
using two wet teaspoons, form the mixture into small log shapes
slice into rounds with a sharp wet knife
place on a damp baking sheet
let cool in refrigerator for 10 minutes
wrap in plastic wrap individually or roll in more toasted sesame seeds

INDEX

BIBLIOGRAPHY

Beer, Maggie (1997), *Maggie's Orchard*, Penguin Books, Australia

Dominé, André (1997), *Organic and Wholefoods*, Konemann, Germany

Downes, John (1978), *Natural Tucker*, Hyland House Publishing, Australia

Downes, John (1983), *Natural Tucker Bread Book*, Hyland House Publishing, Australia

Downes, John (1987), *Soy Source*, Prism Press, Great Britain

Erasmus, Udo (1993), *Fats That Heal, Fats That Kill*, Alive Books, Canada

Grant, Airdre (1997), *The Good Little Cookbook*, MacPlatypus Productions, Australia
(PO Box 5176, East Lismore NSW 2480, airdre@nor.com.au)

Kushi, Michio (1985) *Macrobiotic Home Remedies*, Japan Publications, Inc., Tokyo & New York

Liew, Cheong with Elizabeth Ho (1995), *My Food*, Allen & Unwin, Australia

Oshawa, Lima with Nahum Stiskin (1974), *The Art of Just Cooking*, Autumn Press, Japan

Pitchford, Paul (1993), *Healing with Whole Foods*, North Atlantic Books, USA

Solomon, Charmaine (1997), *Encyclopedia of Asian Food*, Hamlyn, Australia

Weber, Marcia (1992), *Natural Health and Healing for Children*, Simon & Schuster, Australia

Wood, Ed (1996), *World Sourdoughs from Antiquity*, Ten Speed Press, USA

NOURISH

Published in North America by Ten Speed Press
in association with Simon & Schuster (Australia) Pty Limited

Ten Speed Press
Box 7123
Berkeley, California 94707
www.tenspeed.com

First published in Australia in 1999 by
Simon & Schuster (Australia) Pty Limited
20 Barcoo Street, East Roseville NSW 2069

A Viacom Company
Sydney New York London Toronto Tokyo Singapore

Text © Holly Davis 1999
Photographs © Geoff Lung 1999

Library of Congress Cataloging-in-Publication Data on file with publisher.

Project management by Yolande Gray
Design and typesetting by Yolande Gray Design
Photography by Geoff Lung
Food styling by Holly Davis
Styling by Yolande Gray
Props by Sibella Court

Set in Trade Gothic 10pt and Sabon 9pt
Color separations by Response Color Graphics, Sydney
Printed in Hong Kong by South China Printing Co.

1 2 3 4 5 6 7 8 9 10 — 05 04 03 02 01 00

KINDLY SPONSORED BY

Spiral Foods
PO Box 157 Annandale NSW 2038
(02) 9571 9611 Fax (02) 9571 9208

Macro Wholefoods
31-35 Oxford St Bondi Junction.
(02) 9389 7611 Fax (02) 9389 0707
and 170 King Street Newtown
(02) 9550 5422
www.macrowholefoods.com.au

If you would like to be kept informed about

write to
PO Box 192
Newport Beach NSW 2106
Australia
email: hjdavis@ozemail.com.au